An Illustrated History of Quetico Provincial Park

By Shirley F. Peruniak

With Michael Dawber

AF207535

Friends of Quetico Park, 2000
Atikokan, Ont.

© Friends of Quetico Park, 2000
   P.O. Box 1959
   Atikokan, Ont.
   P0T 1C0

Printed by VISTAinfo Canada, Inc.
801 Milner, Scarborough, Ont.

The poem Wilderness by Merilyn Peruniak is used with permission.
Photo on title page taken by Mark Fisher

Photographs in the book are from the John B. Ridley Research Library,
Quetico Provincial Park.
John B. Ridley Research Library
Quetico Provincial Park
108 Saturn Ave.
Atikokan, Ont.
P0T 1C0

Canadian Cataloguing in Publication Data

Peruniak, Shirley F., 1926-
        An illustrated history of Quetico Provincial Park

Includes bibliographical references and index.
ISBN 1-895269-06-7

1. Quetico Provincial Park (Ont.) - History. I. Dawber, Michael.
II. Friends of Quetico. III. Title.

FC3065.Q4P47 2000   971.3'117   C00-930316-2
F1059.Q4P47 2000

Table of Contents

Acknowledgements

Many people have encouraged the assembling of this book. It was the librarian, Andrea Allison, who proposed it to the Friends when she realized that the Historical Photo albums on the shelves in the John B. Ridley Research Library needed a wider audience.

It was the Friends of Quetico Park under chairman Keith Robinson who took on the project and allowed the hiring of editor Michael Dawber.

My promise to those who shared photographs and stories of their days in Quetico that there would someday be a book for sale is coming to be.

I have been encouraged and supported by the Ministry of Natural Resources. Andrea Allison gave many volunteer hours setting up timetables, scanning slides and photographs and looking up details. The Quetico Foundation has supported me in documenting Quetico's history for many years.

On my first canoe trip in Quetico in 1956 I tried to imagine what the first people would have experienced - the trees, the rocks, the water, the animals and all the forces of nature. I wanted to learn their legends of this land. With the coming of the "Teaching Place," aboriginal interpreters with the help of the elders, the chief, councillors and band members perhaps we will.

The albums that I have worked on for many years and from which this Illustrated History of Quetico has come would not have been possible without the help of all the Quetico people, past and present who gave interviews and lent their photographs, and the Station and Interior Rangers who spotted long time visitors with stories to tell.

There was Ted Chisholm, Conservation Officer at Shebandowan who took me to visit Bob Wells on Lac des Mille Lacs. That day we watched a pack of 5 timber wolves gingerly walking over the newly formed ice on that large lake. Tom Nash took me to Calm Lake to interview Ernie Broeffle. Shan Walshe drove me on many an interesting interview trip to the Rainy River, to Wisconsin, to Winton,

Minn. where we stayed with Leone and Bob Hayes. You will meet Bob in the book. Shan had started these albums with his early visit to Bob Readman. Caryl Langford, long time Quetico interior camper from Illinois, has shared her experiences and her writings. Terry Curran took me to Mine Centre to meet Horace Bowes and to listen to his experiences in the logging era. His enthusiasm as he relived some of those times - almost going over Snake Falls - had us on the edge of our seats.

Mike Solomon set up the interview that led to the story of the fire of 1936. It was a stormy May 4 and we drove through a blizzard to meet at the Rendezvous Restaurant in Fort Frances. White caps were smashing in on the shoreline as we listened to Ed Domansky and Lyle Laidlaw tell of their experiences.

I was so lucky to be able to fly with pilots of the Ontario Provincial Air Service in the Piston Otter, and the Beaver. They helped in the collection of their story of flying at Quetico. I met Tom Woodside at the National Aviation Museum in Ottawa where they were restoring an HS2L flying boat and he had flown one over Quetico. Art Colfer is a man of few words but the stories of his lifetime of flying reach back from Quetico to Hudson, Ont. where he flew a plane that was burning and walked out to a road where the first person he met told of seeing a burning plane coming down in the snow on a lake. "That was me" said Art. Bob Grant, as he worked on his own book "Bush flying : the romance of the North" shared information related to Quetico aircraft.

The Regional Directors at Thunder Bay, Lew Ringham, George Elliott and Dr. Don Johnson all gave of their time to provide background and photos. Charles A. Kelly of the Oberholtzer Foundation and his law partner Frank Hubachek kindly lent us photographs. Ray Anderson in International Falls developed negatives from the Oberholtzer Foundation and has taken an interest in our endeavors. He knew Ober well. I thank the Ely Town Office and Columbia Childers for allowing me space and permission to read the early copies of the *Ely Miner* and Bob Hayes who saved the *Ely Echo* for me; Mark Fisher, photographer, gave us his photo of the cliffs south of

Kahshahpiwi. John and Vi Sansted, Mrs. Francis Santineau, Mary Anderson and Elizabeth and Sig Olson all gave of their memories.

On Lac La Croix I thank the friends at Lac La Croix First Nation - the Bosheys, Atatises, Jourdains, Ottertails, Jordans, Geyshicks, and Burnsides. Thanks to Jay and John Handberg for lending old photos and for visits with their mother and father. Further down the lake Bill Zup and Bob Anderson told of the early days. Joe and Vera Meany took me everywhere on the lake and no matter how late we stayed Joe knew the tree line home to the ranger station. Joe's stories of his life have filled a few of the tapes in our collection.

On Basswood Lake I am grateful for the help and the wisdom of Wilbur and Bernice Hyatt, Priscilla and Mike O'Brien, Jon and Marie Nelson, the U.S.F.S. and the Minnesota D.N.R. On Knife Lake Dorothy Molter took time to visit with us.

On Saganaga Lake there were Theresa and Fred Kimberly who told us of the Powells; Rob and Holly Rupert took me to visit Tempest and Irv Benson and the Madsens, Art and Dinna and there was Dorothy, Charlotte, Betsy and Frank Powell. I visited Esther and Mike and Sophie Powell. There were the Blankenburgs, the Andersons, Benny Ambrose and John Bouchard. All these people made us welcome and shared photos and memories. Later, Janice Matichuk and Peter Puddicombe braved the lake with me on stormy days for on-going visits.

Art Madsen's daughter Suzie has put together an album of her father's life as a Quetico Ranger from 1934-1941. Before that Art worked in logging camps and on the logging gators in Quetico.

On Beaverhouse Lake I thank Jon and Marie Nelson who took me to meet the Kielczewskis, an old pioneer family who were on Rainy Lake. When it became "crowded" they moved to Alaska. A book has been written of their experiences. Linda and Vello Laende and Carrie Frechette and Glenn Nolan learned and shared stories of Beaverhouse Lake.

Thanks to Ellen Ripley and Marlene Gagne at French Lake and to Victor Miller, Cheryl Ottertail, Andrew Jourdain, Kalvin Ottertail, Kristen Shields, Natasha McLaren, Jake Splawski, Bill Colvin, George Holborn, and Adrien Van Rooyen.

At Nym Lake and Atikokan there were Janice Niro, Brigitte Tribe, Sheila Hainey, Bettina Siebenmann, George Halemba, Chuck Miller, Dave Maynard, Gary Parker, Dave Lyons, Bob Burns, Pam and Paul Money. John Munroe and Paul Hosick of whom I asked many questions relating to trees always went beyond the call of duty to help me understand.

I was indeed fortunate to be able to talk with Bea Rawn (wife) and Myrtle Rawn Leishman (sister) of Lloyd Rawn, Ross Williams, Dave Elder, Mike Barker, Fergy Wilson and Jay Leather as it was on their shoulders that the running of Quetico rested.

The M.N.R. office in the Whitney Block in Toronto gave me space to read the early Quetico correspondence. Water Resources, Mapping and the Photograph Library knew the Park and located documents that included surveyor diaries, information about the Dawson dams and early photographs.

The Ontario Archives provided us with interviews done in Fort Frances as background for the book *Renewing Nature's Wealth*. Bruce Litteljohn, whose pioneer historical work at Quetico remains an inspiration and whose participation in the logging controversy of the 1970's was so vital, has been a good friend. Wayland Drew shared with us his feelings for Quetico and for wilderness.

I remember the foggy morning when Shan and I set out with historian Gerry Killan, George Warecki and park planner Dave Boggs down Pickerel Lake to introduce them to Quetico about which they were writing. Gerry wrote *Protected Places*, a history of Ontario Provincial Parks and George's thesis *"The Quetico-Superior Council and the battle for wilderness in Quetico Provincial Park 1909-1960"* are both in the John B. Ridley Research Library at French Lake. Thanks for sharing your work with us.

Thanks to the personnel at the Nym Lake Fire Base where people like Bob Cockerline, Mike Horan, Terry Curran and Howard Dupuis located old fire tower diaries and fire reports for us. The fire crews shared vivid stories of their experiences that live on in our files and albums. One crew saved an old Adam Hall stove used by the cook, Don Meilleur, at the 1961 Saganagons fire. To his delight they delivered it to him at his retirement. They also delivered the original stove from the first Cabin 16 to our collection at French Lake.

The Fort Frances staff of the M.N.R. office were always helpful. They lent us space for interviews, told us of former staff who had worked for Quetico. Patti Collett searched every cupboard for Quetico material.

There are over 300 oral tapes in the Research Library and we are grateful to these people; Thora McLure, Arne Korpi, Pentti Aho, George Halemba, Gerry Payne, Joe Kaliska, George Thompson, Ralph O'Donnell, Kay Valley, Borden Fawcett, Bill Beninger, Ken and Martha Kidd, Josephine Ross Kogler.

A special thank you to everyone who donated photographs. Darren Elder helped us with an essential map, and we thank him.

Thank you to Geoff and Jain and Merilyn for all their support.

We welcome corrections and continue to collect stories and pictures. Thank you to those who value Quetico.

Dedication

This book is dedicated to all those who value and help care for Quetico, and especially to the memory of Shan Walshe.

Between Lake Superior and the prairie's edge lies a region known simply as "the Quetico." This is a landscape of tangled lakes and rivers, of rocky islands and towering granite cliffs, of misty mornings and splendid sunsets, of beaver, moose, and loon...

Bruce Litteljohn
Quetico-Superior Country

It is not easy to describe the peculiar charm of Quetico...What gives Quetico its special quality is a unique combination of past and present, history and geography. Here, preserved like a gilded fly in amber, is the Canadian wilderness as the explorers and fur traders knew it centuries ago, the Canada that caught the imagination of Samuel de Champlain and the Chevalier de la Salle, the Canada that David Thompson surveyed and Alexander Mackenzie travelled...

Blair Fraser
Canoe Trails through Quetico

Alone in the wilderness, we learn how foolish are all of mankind's attempts to dominate nature. Quetico teaches this respect. It teaches us that we cannot control the wild because we cannot understand it. It teaches us to accept the mystery of wilderness and to celebrate it. It reminds us that we are forever part of a delicate balance which we can upset but can never improve upon.

Wayland Drew

It is really hard for me to convey the absolutely satisfying experience of spending time in Quetico. The vast stillness in which even the flapping of a loon's wings can be heard soothes my soul...I try to absorb as much peacefulness as I can in order to take "mental mini trips" back here, when...I feel the chaotic confines of civilization. I seem to have the feeling when I leave Quetico that part of me stays here and part of Quetico leaves with me.

J. O'Keefe

Coming a long way from Germany, we found a place as beautiful as we dreamed of or better; did not dare to dream of. We enjoyed it.

W. Miller, Douglas Seleer

Wilderness

dark Quetico islands skirted with silk in
sunset shades   pine regal guarding

before words pictographs experience
of eyes of others   and before then
wilderness in which all wonders were
one glance away

before that glance we knew the breath
of power that inspires all as the apostrophe
of nostril knows the breath the O of mouth
and there was nothing more and nothing
less   no demarcation then of nostril or of
lip   all was one and was a spokeless rimless
wheel a breathing round

we were wild born   we breathed
and were still blind

then in the breathing darkness came
the firefly flash the motherlick of light
that blinked the eye and woke the waiting
mind to wonder

the wheel breathed round   the mind in
wonder dreaming dreaming dreaming
dreamt a wheel

we forged it well   we roll it on and
mark our path with milestones   yet

still we seek to know what we once knew
and are no nearer knowing

and still that wild and wondrous wheel
breathes round one glance

one breath away

Merilyn Peruniak

3

The canoeist does not journey through a trackless wilderness. The canoeist journeys through the past.

Your canoe travels the same route canoes have travelled before. You see the same islands others have seen. You pass the same shoreline others have passed. You walk the same portages others have walked. The cycle of your journey is the cycle of other journeys.

This story is the story of the people who have shared this Quetico cycle, the people who have been drawn to Blair Fraser's "gilded fly in amber." Knowing their history helps us to identify with this place. This will be a journey up the shoreline of Quetico history.

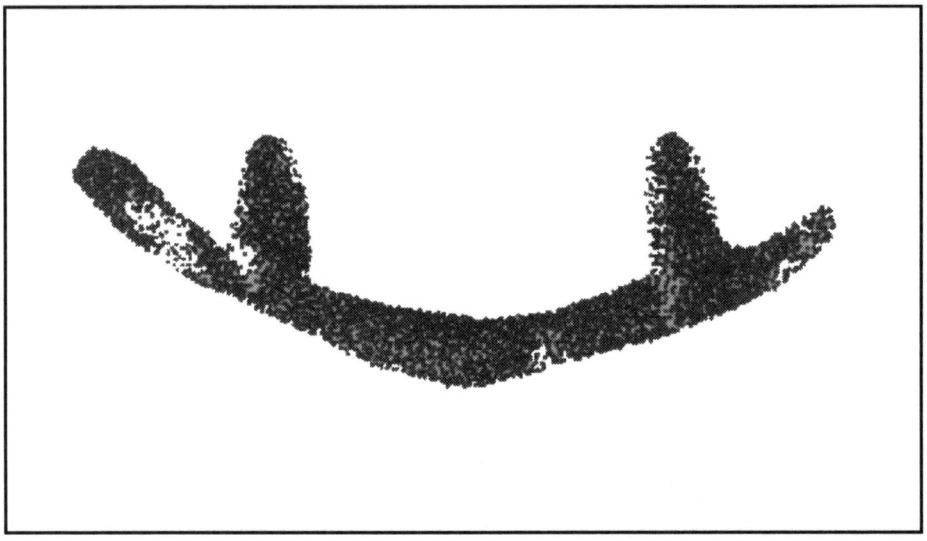

The rock paintings are a link with the past. These places are regarded as sacred by the Ojibwe people and they ask that we treat them with respect. This sketch of one at Trant Lake suggests the way of travel of all of Quetico's visitors.

...and so we continue today.

Our tents and our canoes were copied from the early aboriginal people.

Quetico

The origin of the word "Quetico" is lost in time. It comes from a very old Indian word used to refer to a benevolent spirit whose presence was felt in places of great beauty.

The old Indians did not like to tell the meaning and they differed in how they described the meaning. The elders at Lac La Croix First Nation tell us they use the words "Guetaming" (dangerous) "sagaigon" (water), adding that it is best to travel along the shore.

The name "Quetigo" appears on an 1884 map (published by the Dominion Department of the Interior) showing the country between Lake Superior and the Red River.

Before the Park: Pre-History to 1909

Thousands of years ago, ice, more than a mile thick, covered this area. As it moved, this massive ice sheet scraped away the soft rock and soil, leaving its marks (called "striae") on the harder rock beneath. Imagine the ice, towering a mile over your head!

Slowly, pioneer plants -- like the lichens -- took hold. These lichens began to break down the rock, creating soil for the 'succession' of plants and trees. This succession is still in an early stage at Quetico, and is one of the hallmarks of the park.

The First People may have entered the Quetico area following a land corridor between Glacial Lake Agassiz and Glacial Lake Minong. (Remnants of these remain as Lake of the Woods and Lake Superior.) About 9,000 years ago, a strand line of Lake Agassiz may have been located near "The Pines" beach on Pickerel Lake.

A paleo-point found there is evidence of the aboriginal people's presence. The point is of a unique material -- Hixton silicified sandstone -- found only in Wisconsin (see color insert).

Bare rock covers much of the Park, and in places we can see these scratch marks -- "striae" -- left as the ice moved over the bedrock, picking up and depositing loose material.

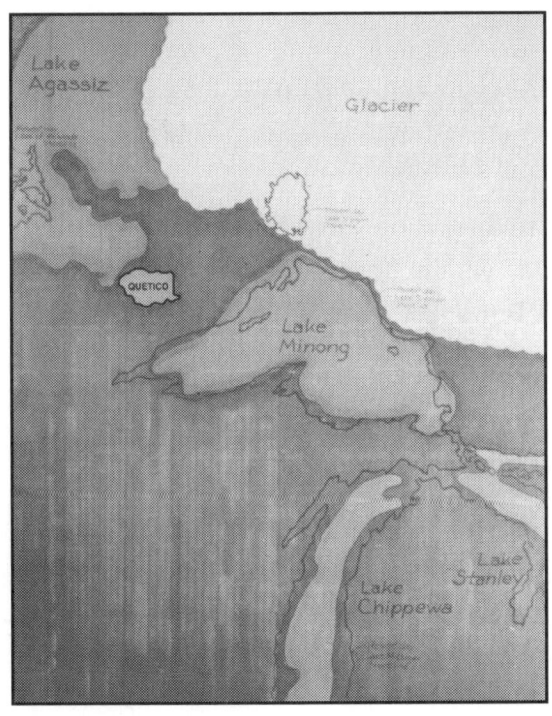

Quetico lay in the land corridor between Glacial Lake Agassiz and Glacial Lake Minong.

The long beach at "The Pines" on Pickerel Lake is a favorite stopping place. Late Paleo-Indian artifacts found here suggest it was a shore-line of Glacial Lake Agassiz -- perhaps the most easterly extension of that lake.

Mounds along the Rainy and Namakan rivers tell of ancient burials, perhaps as long ago as 2000 years. Many modern campsites in Quetico were used by the native woodlands people. As you sit at your campsite, you may find flakes of stone left while they were sharpening their points and tools at this very spot. We respect their presence and must leave them as they were left.

There were two major trading routes passing through Quetico: the Kaministiquia River Route, which began at Fort William (now Thunder Bay): and the Grand Portage Route, which started near the mouth of the Pigeon River on Lake Superior. The Kaministiquia Route passed through the northern and central part of Quetico, while the Grand Portage route hugged what would become the park's southern boundary.

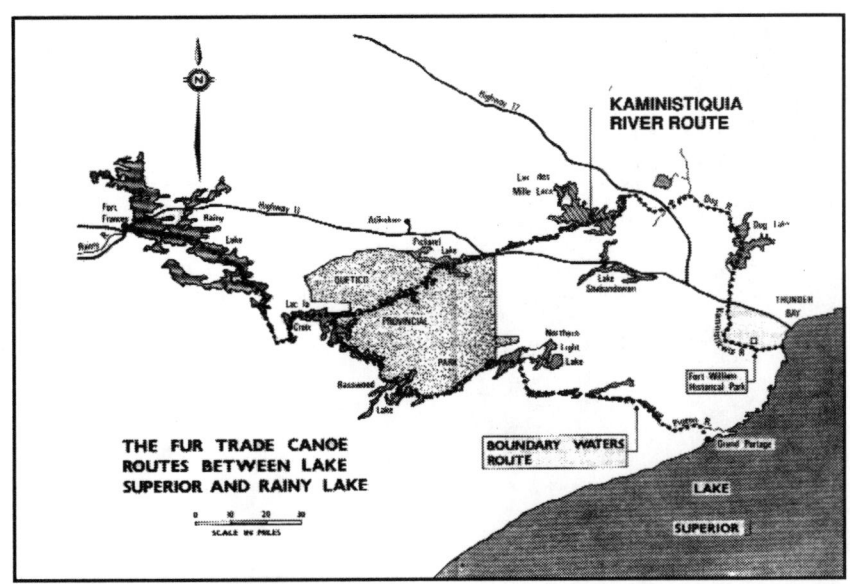

Fur Trade Canoe Routes

The two routes met at the mouth of the Maligne River in Lac La Croix. The Grand Portage had been used by the French explorer La Vérendrye during his first expedition to the Rainy River country in 1731. Many other French traders followed, and a century later, the explorer David Thompson reported there was evidence of an old French fur trading post on Basswood Lake.

Fur traders, their goods and their alcohol changed the way of life of the aboriginal people. The traders, in turn, adopted the native ways of travel and began to learn the language and customs of the native people.

In the early days of the French fur trade, Quetico was a battleground between the Sioux and Ojibwe peoples. The conflict intensified in 1736 after several years of sporadic fighting. Justin Boshey, Chief of the Lac La Croix people from 1982 to 1986, told the story this way: "...this was a great war zone a couple, maybe three hundred years ago...before the whites ever came here. This was once the Sioux nation...Yes, a Sioux nation and the Ojibwe. The Ojibwe found the Sioux and kicked them out of here. Sort of like they needed more hunting area, and so they drove the Sioux west and into the Plains.

9

And this is why you see most of these rock paintings here, and you'll see hills -- sort of like mounds. And there were areas where the Ojibwe have taken over..."

Warrior Hill, also known as Running Rock. Here young braves raced to the top as part of a test to become a member of the Warrior Society of the Ojibwe. From the top a lookout watch was kept for their enemies, the Sioux.

This may have been the time when the Sioux left a warning to the Ojibwe near the well-known "Picture Rock" of Crooked Lake. The explorer Alexander Mackenzie wrote: "Within three miles of the last Portage is a remarkable rock, with a smooth face, but split and cracked in different parts, which hang over the water. Into one of its horizontal chasms a great number of arrows have been shot, which is said to have been done by a war party of the Nadowasis or Sieux [sic], who had done much mischief in this country and left these weapons as a warning to the Chebois or natives, that, notwithstanding its lakes, rivers and rocks, it was not inaccessible to their enemies."

With the fall of Quebec, the French trading posts were soon abandoned, leaving the First Nations people without the trade goods they had grown used to. Benjamin, Thomas and Joseph Frobisher --

well-known fur traders in the Northwest -- reported that the Rainy Lake Indians were destitute of trade goods. The Frobishers' canoes were plundered.

Slowly, the victorious British took the place of the French, exploring deep into the North American interior. In 1775, Alexander Henry may have seen a native village at the site now occupied by Lac La Croix First Nation. The English fur trade continued: in the late 1700s, the Grand Portage route was used by the North West Company, founded by a group of independent fur traders.

The North West Company suffered a setback in 1801, when the American Government threatened to impose duties on British goods crossing the Grand Portage Route. By 1803, the North West traders moved to the more arduous, but all-Canadian, Kaministiquia Route.

Portage across a bridge of two sticks -- known as "Gaa bi maan da we mog" to the Ojibwe. Deux-Rivières Portage.

The "Kam" had first been used by Frenchman Jacques de Noyon in 1688-89 and largely forgotten by Europeans since then. The route was only rediscovered a century later, when local Ojibwe people told Roderick Mackenzie about the Maligne River route to the Kaministiquia.

During those times, the well-known "Deux-Rivières" Portage must have been built. This portage, which begins at Doré Lake, consisted of a log causeway and a bridge. In 1815, Miles Macdonell of the Red River settlement wrote, "This portage is 1300 yards over two hills with a bridge near the middle made by the late Alexander McKay." Scattered remains of the original causeway remain, but the modern portage diverges from its historic path.

In 1821, the powerful Hudson's Bay Company took over the North West Company, redirected fur trading activity north through Hudson Bay -- a cheaper route. After that, the Quetico trade routes fell quiet, and the area saw only sporadic European contact for the next few decades.

The United States and Great Britain did send a boundary survey party through at this time, and they became caught up in the story of John Tanner. As told in *Lake Names of Quetico Provincial Park*, "John Tanner was a white boy, adopted into an Ojibwe family when he was about 10 years old. He lived with them for 30 years, travelling in this area, and on to the Red River. In 1823, he was coming up the Maligne River with his Indian wife and two daughters, in an effort to take the girls out to school." A native friend of Tanner's wife accompanied the party.

As Tanner described (in *The Falcon*), "...at turning a point in a difficult and rapid part of the river, and gaining a view of a considerable reach above...I was surprised that I could see neither him (the Indian man) nor his canoe. ...I was with great effort pushing up my canoe against the powerful current which compelled me to keep very near the shore, when the discharge of a gun at my side arrested my progress...screams of my children drew my attention to the canoe, and

12

I found every part of it was becoming covered with blood...Before I could finish loading (my gun), I fainted and fell on a rock."

Lake Names takes up the story: "Somewhere in the river (believed to be at Tanner's Rapids -- see color insert), he was shot by an Indian, and left to die. The mother deserted him to take the girls back to their Indian home. In great pain, Tanner managed to wade out in the rapids the next day when he heard voices from a canoe in the water above. These men of the Hudson's Bay Co. finally recognized him and took him to Rainy Lake Post, where he was cared for. These events are told in the journals of several expeditions passing over this water route that summer."

The name of Quetico's Tanner Lake still recalls Tanner's story.

In 1846, the artist Paul Kane travelled west with a sketch pad to record the life of what he feared was a vanishing way of life as lived by the aboriginal inhabitants of Canada. This sketch shows the small birch bark canoe they handled so dexterously in the rapids when spearing fish. This could have been drawn below the rapids downstream from the village at Lac La Croix. **[Photograph courtesy of the Royal Ontario Museum, ©ROM]**

Another European who visited the district in that time was Sir George Simpson, the governor of the Hudson's Bay Company. In 1830, Simpson and his bride, Lady Frances Ramsay Simpson, were paddled down the Namakan as Simpson investigated it as an alternative to the route by the Loon River. (They were en route to the Red River Settlement.) Rainy Lake Post, further west, was renamed "Fort Frances" in her honor.

Quetico was in the news in the 1840s, when the U.S. and Britain (acting on behalf of its Canadian colonies) settled the Canada-U.S. boundary in western North America. The boundary had been described in the Treaty of Versailles, which ended the American Revolutionary War. According to that treaty, the international boundary was to follow the water communication between Long Lake and Lake of the Woods. The Pigeon River route was established as this communication.

However, in searching for the most continuous water passage, an American surveyor named Ferguson discovered a water passage further north -- the old Kaministiquia River fur trade route -- and concluded that the boundary should follow *that* continuous water line. The British suggested the St. Louis River system, near Fond du Lac in Minnesota. In dispute, then, was the area long called "Hunter (or Hunters) Island."

Hunter Island

Hunter Island is a name with deep roots in Quetico history. The name was applied to the territory between the Kaministiquia and Grand Portage trade routes. The French called this area "Île des Chasseurs," which may have referred not just to the presence of native hunters, but to a specific family called Hunter. The journal of Dr. McLaughlin of Rainy Lake Post (1823) refers to "one small band, sons of the deceased Chasseur (Hunter)," who trapped near Sturgeon Lake in the wintertime.

The Webster-Ashburton Treaty of 1842 made another attempt to settle the boundary argument. Rejecting both the Kaministiquia and

14

the St. Louis rivers, the framers of the treaty decided the boundary would run along the old Grand Portage fur trade route (*south* of Hunter Island) and thence northwesterly along the Rainy River to Lake of the Woods. Attempts were made by Minnesota spokesmen to question this boundary decision, but the U.S. State Department did not support them.

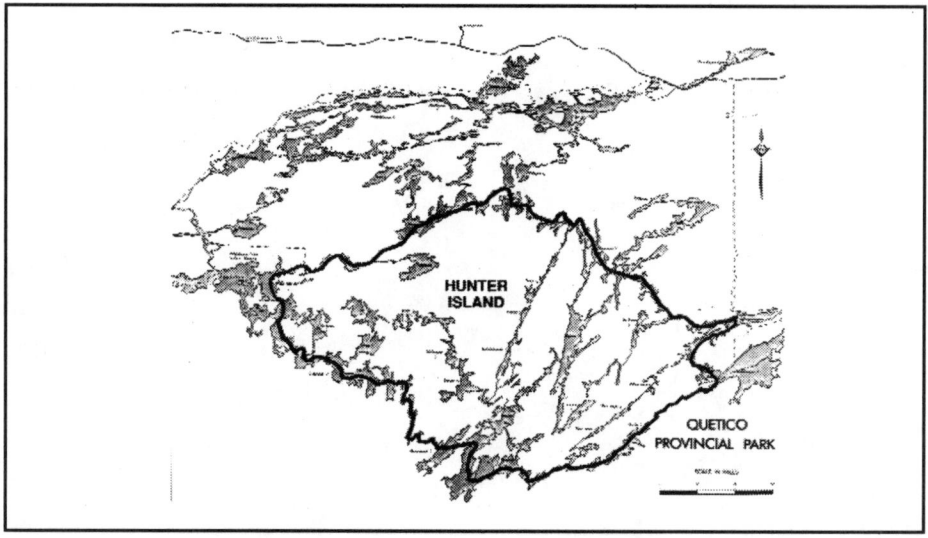

Outline of Hunter Island.

This boundary drew an invisible line through the native communities of the northwest. In 1979, Sophie Powell described how alien this boundary was to her people: "I guess this was all Indian Country in the first place years ago," she said. "The Indians (here) were all one, until the reservations were made. There were no boundary lines. They could go anywhere they wanted. When the boundary line was made they didn't know where it was and they just went back and forth like they had. They were all born in the same place and they didn't know which side to go on. Some sisters belong over on this side and some over on the other side."

The negotiation of Treaty Three in 1873 changed the course of Quetico history. The Ojibwe people of the Northwest ceded more than 80 000 square kilometres of land between Lake Winnipeg and Lake Superior, straddling the modern-day boundaries of Ontario and

15

Manitoba. At the time, these boundaries were in dispute, and would not be settled until 1889. The Province of Ontario did not participate in the Treaty Three negotiations -- the federal government maintained the Treaty Three land was then in the Northwest Territories and, as a result, under direct federal control. This administrative argument would have far-reaching consequences.

Mike and Sophie Powell with family, 1930s. **[Powell Collection]**

The Ojibwe of the Quetico region did not participate in the initial signing of Treaty Three -- three chiefs, including Blackstone of Lac La Croix and Kabaigon of Kawa Bay, signed an "adhesion" to the treaty shortly after. Blackstone then selected territory between the Maligne and Namakan Rivers for a reserve. This is now Reserve 25D (Neguaguon Lake), better known as Lac La Croix First Nation. The name "Neguaguon Lake" is, according to John Boshey Sr., "a whiteman's changed version of the old name, 'shing gook kon ni zog ga ig gun,' which in Ojibwe means 'Lake surrounded by Pines.'"

Stories and legends abound about Blackstone and his family. Until the signing of Treaty Three in 1873, Blackstone moved up and down the travel route (through Quetico) demanding what he believed were the rights of his people. He evicted over-anxious miners, demanded compensation for wood, and expected some tribute from travellers.

Blackstone -- called "Maga day wasin" by his own people -- railed against the Christianization of his people. According to Ojibwe guide Billy Magee, Blackstone once debated religion with the missionaries at Shebandowan. Blackstone is reported to have said, "We are ancient people who may have lived longer than you palefaces. We have our word of God, too. Ours was not in a book, but our laws for life and death are enrolled on these birchbark scrolls. They are sacred to us, as your bible is to you." No Christian mission was established at Lac La Croix. Whenever the people were asked why, the reply was, "Because we had Blackstone."

Blackstone was an eloquent spokesman for his people and took part in the negotiations for Treaty Three in 1873. He was the first chief at Lac La Croix following that Treaty. **[Pencil sketch by Sydney P. Hall, 1881/National Archives of Canada/C-12842]**

Blackstone died in 1885 and was succeeded by his son, Bagitighishig (1885-1889), and then by Waboosweas (1890-1905).

Blackstone's daughter, Shawbogeezigoh, married the son of the Kawa Bay Chief, Kabaigon. She was as storied as her father...once, she was said to have found an orphaned baby bear and nursed it. Her niece, Sophie Powell, said Shawbogeezigoh "was breast feeding one of her babies, so she fed her one baby out of her one breast and the baby bear out of the other breast." Shawbogeezigoh remembered being frightened by the soldiers sent to fight the Riel Rebellion -- the soldiers shared their hardtack biscuits with her.

Shawbogeezigoh at Saganaga Lake in 1945.

Kabaigon chose land at the mouth of the Wawiag River, and this land became Reserve 24C (Kawa Bay). R.B. Ross surveyed both 24C and 25D.

Ross expressed surprise at Kabaigon's choice. Ross wrote in 1877 that there was "...not over two miles that can be cultivated...This reserve is principally rocks and burnt lands. There are no improvements on this reserve, and by the appearance of the place I dont (sic) think the Band frequent it often...You will perceive that this Reserve is not laid off in the usual form, but according to the wish of the Indian sent with me by the Chief, they desired to take only a small plot, south of the Kawawiagamok [Wawiag] River, at the South East corner of the Reserve, behind that being a vast bed of stone, burnt land and fallen timber. As the land was wholly unfit for cultivation I thought better to comply with their wishes." Ross did not understand how rich in plants and animals was the mouth of this river.

In 1878, Ross was much more positive about 25D: "This reserve differs in every respect from the others, being all green bush and about over half of it fit for cultivation. The Indians of the Band seem to be inclined to work and live more on their reserve than any of the other Bands. When I arrived there, I found a number of them busily engaged in putting up a squared log house. They had already a small stable built. They have also five or six acres of land cleared and ready for a crop next year."

Once the land of Treaty Three was given over for settlement, the area was opened up for economic development. The Dawson Trail -- from Lake Superior to the Red River -- made travel possible in a piecemeal, land-and-water way to the West in the 1870s. Its name is a tribute to the man responsible for its creation: Simon Dawson.

Simon Dawson

Simon Dawson was a Scot. As surveyor and cartographer for the Red River Exploring Expedition in 1857, he was involved in the practical aspect of establishing an emigrant route between Lake Superior and Red River. Dawson wrote: "The chief difficulty in the way of rapid transit across the continent lies between Lake Superior and Rainy Lake."

For a brief time, the Dawson Trail would be the first step on a route through Canada all the way to BC. Begun in 1868 under Dawson's supervision, the route consisted of two wagon roads: one from the Lakehead to Lake Shebandowan (about 80 kilometres long), the other from the southwest side of Lake of the Woods to Selkirk on the Red River, which was well over 160 kilometres. Improvements to the old fur trade route served the intervening distance. Small steam tugs assisted with navigation on the larger lakes. (Remains of these tugs can be seen today on Pickerel and Sturgeon lakes.)

The route was a bone-jarring hell and most of it never graduated beyond a rough trail. The 1870 Wolseley expedition reached Manitoba by way of the Dawson Trail -- the expedition was sent to keep the peace and secure Her Majesty's sovereign authority at the time of the métis resistance under Louis Riel in 1870. In October 1873, young men going west to form the Royal Canadian Northwest Mounted Police crossed over the trail in 13 days. In 1876, 1 590 passengers endured its challenges. That was the last year government money was spent on it.

And the railways were coming. By 1875, the American railway from Duluth reached the Red River in Minnesota, where a steamer transported passengers down-stream to Fort Garry in more comfort. Sanford Fleming and his assistant, George Grant, went through the area surveying the route for the Canadian Pacific Railway. During their travels, they met the father of Blackstone near Hungry Hall on the banks of the Rainy River. By 1882, the Canadian Pacific Railway had reached Savanne, north of Quetico, and timber was being leased along its route.

Dawson had moved on to politics and served as a member of the Ontario Legislature -- he was later a Member of Parliament. More than for his political career, he is remembered for his road and for his strong relationship with the Ojibwe people. This was Ojibwe land and, years later, an Ojibwe man told how Dawson sat around their campfires and told stories. Dawson served in negotiations with the native people from 1871 until 1874.

By 1901, William McKenzie and Donald Mann had completed part of their ambitious Canadian Northern Railway through Northwestern Ontario. The *Chronicle-Journal* reported, "On New Year's Eve, 1901, trains left Port Arthur and Winnipeg simultaneously and arrived the following day at their respective terminals. The last spike was driven by both partners at Commissioners Point, 12 miles east of Fort Frances, and on the same day a ceremonial last spike of 'gleaming silver' was also driven at Atikokan by E.J. Davis, Ontario Commissioner of Crown Lands and James Conmee, local MLA."

White prospectors and 'timber cruisers' -- sent to scout potential logging areas -- marveled at the resources of the Northwest. In 1903, one such timber cruiser, L.W. Ayer, wrote in his diary: "We are camped on the south side of Jean Lake on T.B. (timber berth) 48. The timber is at this point the best I have seen in Canada. It is 25% white pine, 46% norway [red pine]."

The largest of the White Pine. They probably saw the earliest French coureur de bois *pass by.*

Lumber companies raced to exploit this resource. In 1900-01, it was reported that "A large amount of pine had been cut during the winter...on the north side of the Seine River at Banning and on up the river. There was a sawmill three miles in from Banning at Calm Lake. One at Little Turtle Lake belonged to the Rat Portage Combine. McKenzie and Mann had a sawmill at Mine Centre." By 1904, the Rainy River Lumber Co. had set up shop under manager J.A. Mathieu -- by 1910, that company split. into several competing interests, including the Backus-Brooks and Shevlin-Clarke operations.

The first provincial crown Timber Agent was appointed in Thunder Bay, and logging licenses were handed out for a mere $2 per square mile along the Canadian Pacific Railway line.

To protect the vast timber resources, Aubrey White, the Assistant Commissioner of Crown Lands, placed Ontario's first fire rangers in the field in 1885. Forest fires were becoming a problem, as sparks from railway engines and human carelessness started a host of fires in the 'slash' left over by logging operations.

In 1888, the first major geological survey of Hunter Island was undertaken. Also in January of that year, surveyor Henry Sewell set out from Port Arthur to survey a north-south meridian from Saganaga Lake. This would become the boundary line between the Districts of Thunder Bay and Rainy River, and (eventually) the original eastern boundary of the park. Near Bitchu Lake, Sewell wrote,

> *"The weather was the most severe it has ever been my lot to experience in this District. Constant heavy snow storms caused complete stoppage of the work on an average of from two to three days each week. There was 4'-6' of snow on the ground.*
>
> *On the west end of Bitchu Lake, the magnetic needle was disturbed indicating, no doubt, valuable mineral deposits.*
>
> *Moose, caribou, bear, small game and fur-bearing animals abound in the country west of Bitchu Lake. There are good sized pine near Bitchu and on Hunter's Island. But the Indians informed me that there was more good pine to the south of the baseline. There are some good groves of spruce and tamarack."*

By 1891, two timber berths had been laid out in the future Quetico. Mines were taking root across the district, though not without controversy. A year before Treaty Three was signed, Blackstone and his warriors drove a party of gold miners from the Moss Lake-Jackfish area.

The Jackfish Gold Mine.

Eventually, the Ojibwe inhabitants of the Northwest were caught up in the mining boom. In 1883, the Indian Affairs *Annual Report* said of the Kawa Bay (24C) people: "Sturgeon Lake Band have scarcely planted anything this year owing to their obtaining constant employment at the Jack Fish Gold Mine. Last winter the women alone chopped 250 cords of wood for the Gold Mining Company so that at present their minds are diverted from raising any crops on the reserves...on June 5 -- only the Chief and his son-in-law were on the 24C Reserve -- the remainder working at Huronian Gold Mine -- Jack Fish Lake. Wasakouse and Waswagikok, sisters of Chief married to American Indians living in U.S. -- drawing annuity for last 10 years from U.S. while Chief drew it for them here. Wasagabowe absent last year -- paid at Grand Portage. Chief would not allow this band to be vaccinated."

Within 15 years, the government reported that the Kawa Bay band was "decreasing every year," even though the people were "fairly prosperous and...self supporting by hunting, fishing, guiding and working in lumber camps." Some of the Kawa Bay people travelled to the hamlet of Savanne to work on the CPR. Eventually, some of those people transferred to the Lac des Mille Lacs Ojibwe band.

It was during this time that North American values underwent a major transformation. As Shan Walshe wrote, "after hundreds of years of regarding the wilderness as an enemy to be exploited and destroyed, some people in the United States and Canada began to have a change of heart, now that they saw the frontier way of life in its death throes. They began to distrust industrialization, fearing that their natural character and strength would disappear along with the wilderness."

Quetico Provincial Park was born in that change of heart. The idea of preserving wilderness, that wilderness had *value* beyond simple economic value, eventually gained respect and support from governments and lawmakers. Two leading figures of the day -- federal minister Clifford Sifton and banker Edmund Walker -- warned that Canada was "spending its forest capital, instead of living off the interest."

The evidence of several government commissions forced the issue. For example, the *Ontario Royal Commission on Game & Fish* (1892) reported "a sickening tale of merciless, ruthless & remorseless slaughter" in Ontario's wild country. The rapid exhaustion of Ontario's pine forests, the working-out of mines, and the decline in fish and game -- which fed the mining and logging camps -- was taking the North down a dead-end trail.

By 1893, Ontario had heeded the words of Alexander Kirkwood and preserved the "gloomy grandeur" of Algonquin as a wildlife preserve. Rondeau, in Kent County, became Ontario's second wildlife preserve in 1894. And in 1898, the province had passed the *Forest Reserves Act*, preserving large tracts of forest in several parts of Ontario. This *Act* declared that, "No land within such (forest) reserves shall be sold, leased or otherwise disposed of, and no person shall locate, settle upon, use or occupy such lands, or hunt, fish, shoot, trap, or spear or carry or use firearms or explosives within or upon such reserves."

Though it had not yet been designated as a Forest Reserve, the province gave some protection to the Quetico. As early as 1895, the government sent rangers out into Quetico to patrol for fires. A.J. McDonald -- a future superintendent of the park -- wrote that, "Everyone in the forest is made aware he is being watched and will be punished if he is responsible for a fire. On every portage route, the proclamations stare him in the face and if he meets a ranger he is handed a pamphlet copy of the *Act*. Squatters and settlers also."

In 1906, four rangers maintained a fire patrol in Quetico during the main fire season. On the shore of Basswood Lake, these rangers built a cabin for themselves on "Johnson's Point" (likely the location now called King Point).

Bob Readman in a canoe at the foot of Silver Falls, outlet of Saganaga Lake, in 1906. **[Readman Collection]**

Robert Readman (1884-1978) was one of the men on the 1906 patrol, and his stories are some of the earliest memories we have of Quetico. Bob got his job as a fire ranger almost by accident, having stopped en route to Vancouver to visit his brother at Fort Frances. Bob was hired in April 1906 and went up into Quetico with his crew. Bob said Quetico was "no man's land" then and even the international boundary was not well defined. If the law was after you, you just crossed the border. Some said there were veterans from the Riel Rebellion who still lived in the area.

He recalled that Ojibwe people from Lac La Croix frequented Kawnipi Lake, and three or four families made a temporary camp at the Kawa Bay Reserve. They found moose, ducks and wild rice in abundance. About 2 1/2 miles up the Wawiag River from Kawa Bay were the remains of buildings and a long wooden flagpole. The Indians said a trading post had operated there years ago.

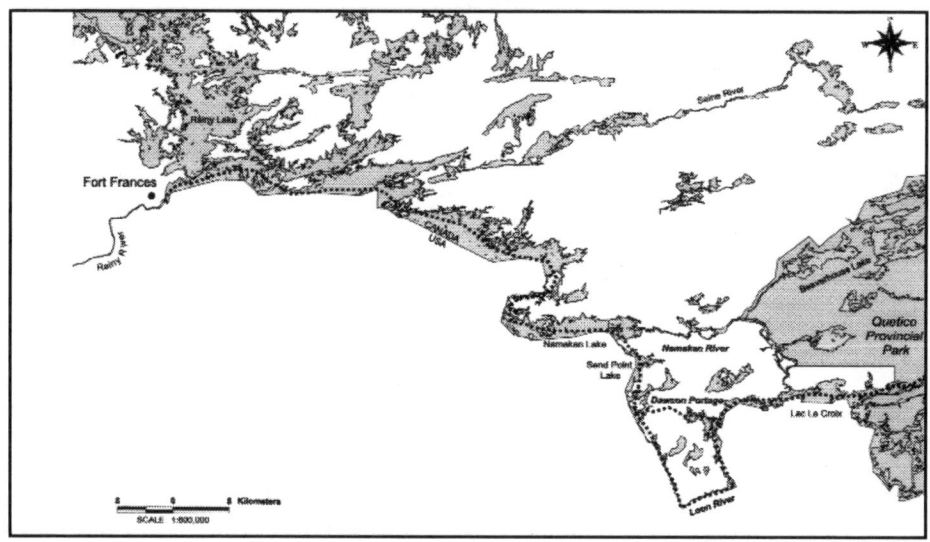

Map showing Loon River & Namakan route.

Bob remembered that the rangers paddled from Fort Frances to Quetico, where they patrolled during the summer season. The rangers preferred the Loon river route into Quetico, rather than facing the swift water on the Namakan.

By the time Bob Readman and his partner canoed the Quetico country, its long-term preservation was already in the works. A co-operative, international effort was underway to save territory on both

26

sides of the Ontario-Minnesota border. On the American side, the Minnesota government reserved more than half a million acres along the 'Boundary Waters,' with the intent to create a fish and game preserve. Christopher Andrews, Minnesota's Forestry Commissioner, urged the government of Ontario to take similar action.

Bob Readman, Chief Fire Ranger, washing clothes on patrol in 1908.
[Readman Collection]

Eventually, the newly elected Conservative government of Sir James P. Whitney became sympathetic. The issue would soon be forced: commercial exploitation of the Quetico forest was imminent, as two timber berths (Nos. 38 and 39) had been leased in the future Quetico Park. Logging was already underway on the American side.

The move to create a new Quetico forest reserve received an important boost in 1907. That year, Ernest Thompson Seton -- the renowned, Ontario-born naturalist -- spoke out in support of a reserve. In 1908, the Member of Provincial Parliament for Rainy River, William Alfred Preston, sought the help of the Canadian Northern Railway in establishing a forest reserve. Preston said he hoped the reserve would protect moose from over-hunting in the summertime. He had recently seen the carcasses of nine moose that had been shot by trophy hunters.

Quetico Fire Ranger Staff of 1908. Among the group are Chief Ranger Bob Readman (3rd from left, bottom row), and next to him on the right, Ephram Crawford, ranger. The fire rangers reported to the Crown Timber Agent, George Watts, on the right. [Readman Collection]

Arthur Hawkes, a public relations man for the Canadian Northern Railway, took up the cause. As Gerald Killan noted, Hawkes "...believed that his company might benefit by promoting the scheme to safeguard and enhance the tourist and sporting potential of the Canadian Northern's Hinterland." He and Preston extracted a promise from the province that Quetico would be saved, if the U.S. took similar action. Aubrey White, the deputy minister of Lands and Forests, took the idea one step further, and declared that Quetico could be made a forest preserve *and* a game preserve.

In his 1908 report, Lands and Forests Minister Frank Cochrane wrote that he was considering creating a forest reserve in "a large block of timber lying on the Quetico River...the estimated quantity of timber on this area is about one and a half billions of feet." (The Quetico River would be the first watershed to be logged after the Forest Reserve was changed to a Park -- a change that permitted logging.) That summer, Cochrane's department assigned 10 fire rangers -- including Bob Readman -- to protect the district from fire. The rangers were paid $75.00 a month for what could be life-and-death work.

While Quetico's future was debated, the boundary between Ontario and Minnesota was under scrutiny yet again. Disputes over the ownership of various islands in Lac La Croix and Lake of the Woods resulted in a joint commission to re-examine the boundary line. The U.S. and Britain (acting for Canada, which did not yet have the power to negotiate international treaties) signed the 1908 Root-Bryce Treaty to settle the issue.

Before the boundary teams set to work mapping the line, the Quetico Forest Reserve became a reality. Not only would Quetico be preserved, but -- in a remarkable, cross-border effort -- a vast portion of northern Minnesota would also be protected. The efforts of Christopher Andrews, W.A. Preston, Arthur Hawkes, and many others were rewarded.

Aubrey White, Assistant Commissioner of Lands and Forests, 1887-1905; Deputy Minister of Lands and Forests, 1905-1915.

29

On 13 February 1909, in one of his final acts as President of the United States, Teddy Roosevelt created the Superior National Forest. Almost simultaneously, the State of Minnesota established the Superior Game Refuge, including more than 1.2 million acres of land in the boundary country.

The Ontario government acted on the advice of Aubrey White, who wrote:

> *"The undersigned has the honour to state for the information of the Minister that representations have been made to the Department to the effect that the Federal Government of the United States, and the Government of the State of Minnesota propose withdrawing from sale or disposition a considerable tract of territory in the State of Minnesota and forming it into a forest and game preserve. So that the timber might be preserved, and that there should be a harbor for game.*
>
> *It has been urged that Ontario should set apart territory immediately adjoining as a forest and game preserve. By this means, a very large area would be preserved from destruction, and game would flow freely between the two reserves, the international boundary being a water one.*
>
> *The undersigned, having given the matter careful consideration, has the honour to submit the annexed map and description showing the territory, which he is of opinion might be set apart as a forest and game reserve. The Minister will observe that the area covered is about one million of acres; that it is well watered, and that the boundaries are easily defined, the larger proportion of them being water. The undersigned begs leave to point out that the reserve covers the celebrated Quetico region, which contains one of the largest bodies of pine timber in the Province. It is estimated that*

on the territory proposed to be set aside there is about one and a half billions of red and white pine, five millions or cords of pulpwood, besides quantities of tamarac [sic] and other merchantable woods. The danger to which this timber is exposed has been a source of anxiety to the Department for some time, although a staff of fire rangers has been placed in it from year to year. The undersigned has always felt that some closer and more intelligent supervision of this territory should be made. The undersigned is, therefore, of opinion that this territory should be created into a forest reserve and withdrawn from sale or settlement. There is no agricultural land in the territory proposed to be set aside. It is not believed to be mineral bearing, the only known discovery being an indication of iron at the South East end, where some mining locations have been sold and patented. There are two Indian Reserves in the territory. The Indians would not be interfered with, and their sympathy could be obtained by employing them occasionally as fire rangers, as has been done in the Temagami Reserve. The setting aside of this new forest reserve would only be another step in the direction of conserving and protecting an additional large body of pine, and therefore in accord with the general policy of the Government. The undersigned submits this memorandum for the information of the Minister, and commends to his favourable consideration the setting apart under authority of the Forest Reserves Act of a Reserve to be known as the Quetico Forest Reserve, as described on the plan and description hereto annexed. The undersigned is of opinion that a Chief Ranger should be appointed for this Reserve, and an adequate staff of rangers placed under him so as to protect the timber from destruction by fire."

A few weeks later, on 01 April 1909, the Ontario cabinet approved an Order-in-Council creating a forest reserve in the "celebrated Quetico region." The Order-in-Council stated that Quetico should be "withdrawn from location settlement or sale and kept in a state of nature as far as that is possible, and that a staff should be created under a chief ranger to guard the timber from destruction by fire..."

The first step had been taken.

Wilderness Voices: Ernest Oberholtzer and Billy Magee

Ernest Oberholtzer. [Oberholtzer Collection]

Ernest Oberholtzer -- "Ober" -- was a driving force of the conservation movement for most of his 93 years. Iowa-born, Ober fought to preserve the Quetico-Superior wilderness on both sides of the border. The modern parks of this region stand as testament to his efforts. He spent much of his life among the Ojibwe people, recording their stories and legends. While he travelled and lived on other continents, the north country was truly his home: he once wrote that moving to Rainy Lake was "one of the dreams of my life." His life was lauded as being "like a strong bright thread (running) through the fabric of many accomplishments."

Quetico captured Oberholtzer's imagination. In a 1964 interview with Bruce Litteljohn, Ober said: "Quetico in 1909 seemed to be a primitive country, a wonderful place, and it was no wonder the Indians had traditions and felt spirits in there. It had a spirituality. You felt you were in a kind of magic land."

Billy Magee. [Oberholtzer Collection]

Ober's story became part of Quetico's story from the first. In the summer and early fall of 1909, Ober took a canoe trip into the newly-established Quetico Forest Reserve. As his guide, Oberholtzer chose Billy Magee, an Ojibwe guide who has become as much a Quetico legend as Ober. Magee -- known as Taytahpahwaywiton ("Far Distant Echo") to his own -- was from the Seine River Reserve, west of Quetico. For two dollars per day, Magee agreed to take Oberholtzer through the Forest Reserve and along the boundary waters as far as Gunflint Lake, east of the modern park boundary.

Oberholtzer's diary of that journey is a snapshot of Quetico at the moment of its preservation.

August 22, 1909: "One of the finest campsites that I have ever seen is on the point of the island where one turns west for the portage to Beaverhouse. Grove of Norways on dry level sandy shore; several miles of perfect sand beach. R.E. Readman of Fort Frances had a very fine camp."

Ernest Oberholtzer and Billy Magee met Chief Ranger Bob Readman cooking his dinner on patrol in 1909. [Oberholtzer Collection]

August 23, 1909: "Just above the entrance to Wolseley Lake the river branches, and at the entrance to the north branch there is a splendid torrential fall swinging round a low curved canyon. Island at the mouth. Beautiful lichen covered cliffs on the north side. Near the portage just at the foot of the falls the Indians have erected some stands of poles from which they spear sturgeon with a long rod."

August 24, 1909: "Eight chain portage in the run round Snake Falls which is a series of twisting turbulent rapids without any distinction of land forms. A mile or so further we came in sight of the big gray lake lying like the harbour of an ocean, where one would expect a lighthouse on the capes...birchbark canoes passing each other at the inlet. Indian village of cedar houses, and bark wigwams."

34

*George Katz, a fire ranger on the Maligne River wood dam in 1906. The 96-metre dam was built in 1873 by Simon Dawson to raise the water in the creek up to the Deux-Rivières portage -- this facilitated steam tug navigation. [**Readman Collection**]*

August 27, 1909: "The Maligne Dam is still intact, though very old. Large Indian camp on the portage, stands to dry sturgeon. Billy said there used to be a Hudson Bay post on the hill above the dam. A little farther is another rapid where we were just about to portage when we saw two canoes of fire rangers coming down. They both shot the rapids without difficulty and we had a long talk together afterwards. One of the canoes contained Wm. Martin and R.E. Readman; the other held Walt and his chum."

September 6, 1909: "Reached Poohbah at half past six and was very tired. Fortunately we had had a perfect day and we now had a perfectly clear night with the sky abloom with stars. They made a good deal of light and some of them threw long spiral reflections upon the water. I had to finish pitching the tent in the dark on site of a large old Indian wigwam. Billy said the Indians had been making canoes there and that it was a favourite lake for that purpose. The Indian name of the lake is Gan dook gwe mawitay..." (The original name -- which means "place for getting bark for canoes" -- is still remembered by some of the Lac La Croix people. The current name, Poohbah, has no meaning here.)

Drying racks for fish and meat: sturgeon drying. **[Bill Magie Collection]**

September 7, 1909: "On the way, behind an island, we saw a cow moose and calf feeding in the middle of the stream. The calf swam clear across from one shore to another and I stood on the island within thirty feet of where he came ashore. The strong wind from his direction prevented him from smelling me and I should probably have had a very fine picture if I had not stepped out too soon. As soon as he saw me he jumped as if he had been shot and disappeared in the bush. ...His mother, in the meantime, was feeding most luxuriously all unconscious of what had happened. Billy and I paddled right beside her before she saw us."

September 11, 1909: "Went down the north shore of Kahnipimenanikok from point to point and near the entrance to McKenzie Lake met an Indian man and woman in a canoe. They had a blanket for a sail and were going along well with the wind. They said

Moose. [Oberholtzer Collection]

they had just lost a child a few days before....On Saganagons Lake there used to live an old Indian named 'Kay pay quin.' He had a very large family -- seven children. He was chief of all the Indians on Kahnipiminanikok." ('Kay pay quin' is Kabaigon, first Chief of the Kawa Bay people. He died in 1885.)

A birch bark canoe with a blanket sail on Kawnipi Lake. [Oberholtzer Collection]

Oberholtzer and Magee had several encounters with other native people on their journey. On 17 September, they met Leo Chosa, a trader who kept a small store about a mile from the old Hudson Bay post at Inlet Bay. (Chosa will appear again in our story.) Chosa told Ober he had spent five winters on the north side of Hunter Island and had done very well. The most plentiful animal was the mink, he said.

The next day, the travellers passed two canoes of Indians in the Basswood River. They were from Lac La Croix and were on their way to get supplies for winter trapping.

Throughout the journey, Magee was reluctant to share his stories with Oberholtzer, though he did relate that the many pictographs in Quetico were all done by one medicine man -- Omo ("Bee") -- a thousand years ago. Towards the end of the trip, Magee relented and told Ober the history of the 'black sturgeon,' a story still told among the Lac La Croix people in the 1980s.

Leo Chosa and his gasoline fishing boat used on Basswood Lake in 1912. This is the old fish dock at the Hoist Bay end of the four-mile railway portage. They used to haul their fish over the railway and down to Winton on Fall Lake. **[Bill Magie Collection]**

This journey began Ober's association with Quetico, and our debt is to him for a lifetime of work.

The Ojibwe people from Lac La Croix often travelled to Basswood Lake where they would camp. There were relatives at Jackfish Bay and a logging railroad to help them go for supplies at Winton. **[Bill Magie Collection]**

Sigurd Olson -- another famous advocate of conservation -- eulogized Ober in the 19 June 1977 edition of the *Rainy Lake Chronicle* as "a man with a dream...no one will ever forget [his] tales of the Black Sturgeon, Manitou, and Nanibougou who lived in the depths of the lakes he knew. ...If anyone wishes to describe Ober, it would be as one who loved wilderness for he believed a world without wild places where man could commune with God and Nature was meaningless. He left us a rich heritage of courage, love, and dedication to the dream he carried in his heart until his passing."

Forest Preserve to Park: 1909-1913

In Quetico's first year, 1909, the province reported:

The Quetico Reserve, in the Rainy River district, the latest addition to our list of forest reserves,--suffered somewhat from forest fires during the past summer. As this reserve is away from settlement and railways, or lumbering, it was difficult to account for the fires, unless they had crossed from the Minnesota side, where serious fires raged for considerable periods. We had an adequate staff of rangers on duty in this Reserve, and every effort was made to protect it.

In the fall of 1909, Bob Readman and Ephram Crawford were appointed Park Rangers for Quetico. By an extraordinary coincidence, both men were from Gravenhurst, in Muskoka District, but did not know one another. Together, they built what was probably the park's first ranger cabin, near the future site of Cabin 16. (Cabin 16 was long an entry station on Quetico's southern border.) During the following winter, Crawford and Readman patrolled the Quetico boundary for American poachers -- several were caught and fined.

Readman and Crawford were also under instructions to evict any Indians they found on Hunter Island that winter. The needs of the First Peoples of the area and the policy of wilderness conservation came into conflict, as they would many times in the future.

This eviction was criticized by Leo Chosa, the trapper, commercial fisherman and trading post operator who met Ernest Oberholtzer and Billy Magee in 1909. Chosa, a man of mixed French-aboriginal ancestry who worked on the American side of Basswood Lake, wrote a stinging letter to the Canadian government, demanding to know why the Indians were being removed. "Why did not the government notify them during the summer?" he asked, "When they could easily have located outside the Forest Reserve, Or made some shelter for their families on their own reserve? But this driving them off in the middle of the winter does not appear to me as being an action worthy of a civilized people."

With the creation of the Quetico Forest and Game Preserve, two park wardens, Bob Readman and Ephram Crawford, were appointed to stop hunting or trapping in the reserve. Here Ephram Crawford is camped at Poohbah Lake in the fall of 1909, while on the first winter patrol in Quetico. [Readman Collection]

J.D. McLean, an Indian Affairs official, replied that "The Department is confident that, as Hunters Island has been set apart as a forest reserve, whereon the game is specially protected, the Ontario Government will not grant Indians permission to remain on the reserve, as it would be understood that they would while there kill sufficient game for their support." The evictions stood. (These events would be referred to in the apology given to the Lac La Croix First Nation by the Ontario Government in 1991.)

In spite of their orders, relations between the rangers and the Ojibwe people seemed good. "Bud" Gadd -- son of an early Quetico ranger, Harry Gadd -- writes that his father's "mention of the Indian people seemed to centre around a 'Chief Ottertail' whom he held in high regard. He told of 'smoking the peacepipe' with this man telling me what a fine man he was...Friendly terms seemed to prevail between rangers and the Indian band it did appear. Part of the duty of a ranger was to see that no one pilfered items of value from the Indian people or tampered with the gravesites..."

*John Ottertail of Lac La Croix, who acted as guide to the Commission in the Quetico Forest Reserve. [**Final Report of the Ontario Game and Fisheries Commission, 1909-1911**]*

Having protected the vast Quetico wilderness, the province wanted to gauge the health of the game and fish in the region. Recalling the "slaughter" reported by the 1892 Royal Commission, the Ontario Game and Fisheries Commission travelled to Quetico in the summer of 1910 (or 1911) to investigate. Specifically, the Commission inquired whether the increased human population of the North was putting pressure on fur-bearing animals.

*Tracking in the Quetico Forest Reserve. [**Final Report of the Ontario Game and Fisheries Commission, 1909-1911**]*

Game and Fisheries Commissioner Kelly Evans was impressed by Quetico, but not by the province's efforts to protect it. The province had protected the forest of Quetico, but not its inhabitants. The Commission's report said, "...the Department of Lands and Forests had placed a mere ten rangers working in pairs in the Quetico, who, for only five months of the year, had the impossible task of patrolling the reserve's 1500 square miles. The rangers keep to the larger rivers and lakes and remain in blissful ignorance of the geography of their beats and undertake or attempt but very little work. Consequently, local hunters and trappers enjoy relatively unrestricted access to Quetico's resources, especially during winter."

The report led to the establishment of more regular patrols. In 1910, more permanent ranger stations were built, and in 1911, the province appointed a Warden to oversee the Forest Reserve. The choice added another legendary name to the Quetico story: Colonel Young.

Colonel Young

David Douglas Young was not a man of small measure. Tall and well built, with a soup-strainer mustache, Young was the image of the Canadian soldier. He was also a frontiersman of great experience, experience that would be put to good use in his 'retirement!'

Born in 1857, Young entered the military at age 26. He served for more than 25 years, eventually becoming second-in-command of the Yukon Field Force in 1897. Quetico ranger Bob Readman well remembered Young's stories of the Yukon in the Gold Rush days -- including such extraordinary feats as the Force's march from the Stikine country of British Columbia to the Yukon's Teslin Lake.

Colonel D.D. Young in a soldier's uniform before he came to Quetico Park. He was Chief Warden of the Quetico Forest Reserve from 1911 to 1913. ***[Public Archives of Canada/C-8061]***

The Force continued on to Dawson to assist the Mounted Police during the mining rush.

Young eventually retired from the military in April 1911, and was named as Quetico's first Warden by the province.

One of the park rangers, Bill Darby, met the new Warden at Quetico Station (on the Canadian Northern Railway) and took him by canoe to French Lake. During the summer of 1911, Young and his rangers -- including Bob Readman, Jock McDonald and Bert Lock -- took a canoe trip through the Reserve. They found signs of illegal trapping south of Quetico Lake, and destroyed trappers' shacks and traps. They also met people from the U.S. who had been visiting Quetico for years.

Quetico Station on the Canadian Northern Railway. **Photo taken in 1993.**

Of his charge, Young said: "The Quetico Game Reserve is one of nature's most beautiful spots with nature unadorned. The lakes and waters cannot be surpassed in beauty, and forests in their true light...I consider it will be the greatest tourist recreation resort and fisherman's paradise on the continent." Young drew this conclusion after conducting a tour of inspection in 1911.

45

*Park rangers Henry Bone (bow) and Bill Darby in 1912. **[Bill Darby Collection]***

*At the top of the Maligne River in 1911. Bert Lock, Colonel Young and Jock McDonald examine the boiler and engine from a steamer used on the Dawson route. **[Readman Collection]***

Under Young's direction, Quetico's first true park facilities were built. In 1912, Young and rangers Harry Gadd, Fred Hampshire, Milt Adams, Bob Johnston, and Stuart Campbell constructed a men's bunkhouse, two outbuildings for storage, a stable, and a small office. All of the supplies had to be brought overland from the railway station at Kawene, north of the Reserve, and a trail was cut between Kawene and French Lake to ease transportation. (The 'ease' was minor -- the trail was infamously rough and difficult!) The rangers also cleared four acres of land, and planted a garden to supply vegetables.

Jock McDonald, Colonel Young, Robert Readman, and Bert Lock sitting in front of a canoe and tent beside Lac La Croix in 1911. ***[Readman Collection]***

The progress was great -- but insufficient for the Game & Fish Commission, which was quite critical of the province's efforts. The Commission wrote: "...it is apparent that if the reserve is to fulfill its functions and to be conserved to posterity, greater expenditures will have to be devoted to the maintenance of a more adequate staff to protect it." Young reported, indeed, "there is a great deal to be done yet." He also recommended the Reserve be expanded out to Windigo Station on the CNR, west to the hamlet of Banning, and then south to the International Boundary. It would not be the last discussion about Quetico's borders.

*Jock McDonald and Bert Lock with Colonel Young in the middle on Lac La Croix on their way to Bottle Portage in 1911. [**Readman Collection**]*

*Colonel Young in the stern and Mrs. Young in the middle of the canoe (1911-1913). [**William Thompson Collection**]*

The Commission asked for ranger posts to be established at Lac La Croix, Quetico Lake (on Eden Island), at Pine Portage near Pickerel Lake, and at the east end of Basswood Lake. During 1912, Quetico's rangers built patrol shacks at Sturgeon Narrows, Tinsley's Point (King Point?), Lac La Croix, and Eva Lake. They also took possession of several fire ranger cabins, on Eden Island and on Basswood Lake, and spent part of the summer cutting portages.

Far away from the pines, in Toronto, the Game & Fish Commission had spurred more government action to protect Ontario's dwindling fish and game stocks. In the spring of 1913, the government of Sir James Whitney brought in new, more muscular legislation -- the *Provincial Parks Act* -- which outlawed hunting (except in rare circumstances) and required sport fishers to have a license. The park rangers were given all the powers of a police officer. However, the bill also permitted the Minister of Lands, Forests & Mines to issue timber licenses in parks.

Having only just become a Forest Reserve, Quetico was now about to be 'converted' into a Provincial Park. In October 1913, the government reported Quetico was being considered for park status, and by December, the change was put in motion. By Order-in-council, "the territory comprised in the Quetico Forest Reserve...be withdrawn from sale, settlement, and occupancy...and be reserved and set apart as a public park and forest reserve, fish and game preserve, health-resort and fishing ground, for the benefit, advantage and enjoyment of the people of Ontario and for the protection of the fish, birds, game and fur-bearing animals therein..."

On 08 December, Colonel Young -- the first (and last) Warden of Quetico Forest Reserve -- handed over control to A.J. McDonald, the first Superintendent of Quetico Provincial Park.

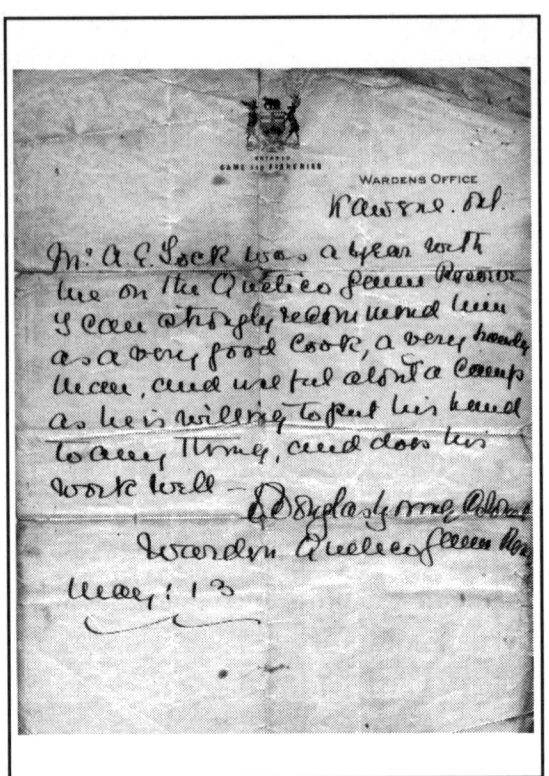

Colonel Young's recommendation of Bert Lock.

A.J. McDonald: 1913-1917

When A.J. McDonald arrived at Kawene from Cochrane as Quetico Superintendent, he took on one of the most daunting jobs imaginable. He had to manage this vast wilderness park -- stop fires, catch poachers, issue licenses, create portages -- with about a dozen men and a handful of supplies. When Col. Young departed, the province reported it did not know "what he had in the way of stores on hand, a pair of ponies, waggon [sic] and sleigh..."

McDonald set about his task. He was, in the words of ranger Bill Darby, "A level-headed man, he was on the up and up."

McDonald observed his charge first hand, on the ground. In 1914, McDonald reported: "There are many moose and deer in the north and west sections. Reports of wanton slaughter of moose near the American border have come to us. There are foxes, coyotes, wolves and skunks in the woods. Beaver are increasing, there are mink, some otter and a plentiful supply of weasels. Bear sign is numerous and on June 2 moose calves were killed by bears at Pickerel L. Porcupine are bad in the pine timber. Bass have been found in two lakes only."

One of McDonald's first projects was the construction of the Park Headquarters at French Lake. E.P. Lawrence put up the building during the summer of 1914. McDonald reports: "The headquarters are on the east shore of French Lake at the west end of what is known as the French Portage." This building would house the park's administration until the Second World War.

*Park Headquarters at French Lake. [**Bob Halliday Collection**]*

Superintendent A.J. McDonald (middle front) with his rangers at the 1914 election day. Sam Boone is sitting on the far right and Bill Rooney is standing between A.J. McDonald and Sam Boone. ***[Boone Collection]***

Cabin 16 on Basswood Lake in 1912. ***[Bill Darby Collection]***

McDonald's men worked under almost any conditions. "I insisted on my rangers being constantly on patrol and on the lookout for fires," McDonald wrote, "especially during the dry season from May until Sept. when tourists are canoeing in the park." The winter was no relief: when ranger Bob Oglestein suffered snow blindness in April 1914, he was brought in from the bush and put to work hewing logs for new park buildings.

Many logs went into the park's ranger cabins, and the cabins soon became one of the cornerstones of Quetico's operation. Quickly and simply built by two or three men, these huts served as human outposts throughout the park. In the early days, A.J. McDonald reported that, "All new huts built are 16' by 20' of hewn and peeled logs, with pitch roof covered with paroid [sic] roofing, well floored and contain bed, stove, table and benches or stools. They are made warm and comfortable and kept clean by the men."

*Four fire rangers at the park ranger Cabin 19 at Lac La Croix, near Twin Falls. Mamie Gustason, shown wearing a hat, was a visitor in 1919. [**Bill Darby Collection**]*

53

Ranger Bill Darby in his red canoe in front of old Cabin 16 on Basswood Lake. [Bill Darby Collection]

One of the best-known of these warm, comfortable retreats was Cabin 16, on Ranger Island in Basswood Lake. In 1913, ranger Bill Darby was sent to patrol Basswood, along the park's southern boundary. As a base, he used a simple hut -- eventually dubbed "Cabin 16." (The ranger cabins in the park were numbered in sequence.) At a time before airplane patrols or motor boats, his red canoe became a familiar unwelcome sight to local poachers.

The Quetico rangers were still citizens, even in this far away place. In June 1914, ten of them dutifully voted for Conservative J.A. Mathieu in that summer's provincial election. Mathieu's Liberal opponent, Richard Langstaff, received no votes at Quetico Provincial Park. The *Fort Frances Times* remarked, "It is a matter of public talk the open manner in which some of the Prov. and Dom. Gov't officials came out and worked against Mr. Mathieu, the gov't candidate...general feeling there will be several vacancies as a result."

The First World War also touched Quetico. McDonald said, "Two of my rangers have enlisted during the past season, one of whom [Jeff Lefroy] was severely wounded in the battle of Langemarck, in France." Lefroy went back to the front, and McDonald said, "he was a very good man in this service." Rangers Herb Rooney and William Rooney also enlisted at Port Arthur. McDonald complained about the war's impact on his park: "Owing to the war and consequent scarcity of men in this vicinity during last summer it was almost impossible to secure sufficient suitable men to patrol the park properly. Men who would suit on land patrols along railroads and cut-over limits would not do here, as all of our travelling has to be done by canoes, and a man who is not a canoeman is useless in Quetico."

McDonald described that last summer before the War:

"During the trapping season my men travel in pairs patrolling the sections over which they have charge to prevent illegal trapping and hunting. I feel that I have a good staff and that they have done excellent work this season, when it is considered that they had to undergo many hardships in getting things into shape, did so without shelter huts or trails, and had to portage outfits and supplies through snow and over rough ground. I do not consider that much illegal trapping was done last season. We picked up some steel traps along the boundaries and destroyed several deadfalls, presumably set by Indians. I have told my rangers to endeavor to keep on good terms with our Canadian Indians but warned them of American Indians coming across to trap in Canadian territory."

The invisible line continued to divide sister from sister.

McDonald said the 'Canadian Indians' were spending time at Lac La Croix: "There are no Indians at Reserve 24C near the eastern boundary, but quite a few on Reserve 25D at the mouth of the Namakan river. They do not seem to cultivate any portion of the Reserve, but subsist by hunting and fishing." Around that time, the chief of the Kawa Bay people, Nanekaconap, died -- the story often told is that he died while pulling a toboggan over the ice. Nanekaconap may have been buried at Agnes Lake: a well-kept, fenced burial plot could be seen there for many years, and people around the park still recall seeing this grave. (No trace of it remains.)

*The grave that was on Agnes Lake years ago. It may have been the grave of Kawa Bay Chief Nanekaconape (Ninagaconeb), who died in 1915. [**Bill Darby Collection**]*

The Kawa Bay Reserve came under scrutiny in 1915, when the province finally transferred the reserves created by Treaty Three to the federal government. The lands had been in dispute for years. Aubrey White wrote:

> *"At the time the treaty was made the western and northern boundaries of the Province of Ontario had not been definitely determined, and upon the assumption that the territory affected was part of the Northwest Territories and under the control of the Dominion Government, that Government authorized the laying out of certain reserves for the Indians...When the boundaries of Ontario were legally established by the judgment of the Imperial Privy Council, Ontario's title to all the lands within her boundaries was undoubted.*

As Ontario had not been consulted in connection with the making of the treaty or the selection of the reserves the Government declined to recognize what had been done..."

Indian wigwam of stretched moose hide at Kawa Bay, 1915. **[Bill Magie Collection]**

After talks between Ontario and the Dominion, the Lac La Croix Reserve and all other Treaty Three reserves were acknowledged, except for Reserve 24C -- 24C was "not confirmed" by Ontario. The province maintained it had already given the land required to meet the obligations of Treaty Three in Ontario. The fact that 24C was inside a Forest Reserve was also an issue for the province. Ontario and the Dominion reached a deal to abandon 24C in December 1913, and this was confirmed by the Ontario legislature in April 1915. The federal government later paid the province about $23,500 for "excess area in Treaty Three."

These actions remain controversial.

By 1918, only five people remained on the Treaty List for Kawa Bay: the widow of Kabaigon, the widow of Nanekaconap, Pokonakeyickquiape, Little Moose, and Maningatai.

American tourists were now venturing into the Quetico wilderness. In August 1915, four men from Falls City, Nebraska, canoed the park and its American sister. The diary of that trip contains some fascinating stories...

In August 1915, four gentlemen from Falls City, Nebraska, travelled for 30 days in the Quetico-Superior wilderness. **[Bill Magie Collection]**

"Aug 10. Crossed the portage from Loon Lake to Lac La Croix where James Beatty lived. He had a reputation for being the strongest man in the north and was for years the game warden and deputy forester for Minnesota. He is now a fisherman and a trapper.

At the portage [now called Beatty Portage], we met a party of Canadian engineers who were surveying and plotting an official map and boundary line of the lake for their government."

"Aug 18. We started across Crooked Lake at 7 am and were lost three times before noon and as many times after, and camped at night on a river branch of Crooked Lake as totally ignorant of where we were as anyone could be."

United States Boundary Survey base-measuring party en route to camp on Basswood Lake in January 1916. Bill Darby is second from left. ***[Report: International Boundary Commission: Re-establishment of the Boundary Between the United States and Canada--Northwesternmost Point of Lake of the Woods to Lake Superior, 1931]***

Of the park rangers, the diary says: "The rangers were gentlemen who seemed to take pride in the service they were doing. They were strict, prompt and severe with the violators of the forest and game laws of their country."

We have another invaluable snapshot of those early days at Quetico. In late 1916, the editor of the *Fort Frances Times* and *Rainy Lake Herald*, J.A. Osborne, visited the park at the invitation of A.J. McDonald. Osborne reported his trip in great detail:

> *"We left Fort Frances on the midnight train arriving at Kawene where we were met by Mr. McDonald. Here we took our packsack and walked over a fairly good road 1 3/4 mile to Eva Lake, where a gasoline launch*

was waiting to take us across and down Eva Lake to French Lake portage, a distance of 7 miles. The journey down this beautiful lake was truly magnificent, the deep autumn tints of the birch, poplar, maple, ash and other trees contrasting with the deep green of the pine and spruce making a beautiful picture especially along the shore and in narrow passages of the lake where the placid waters like one huge mirror, reflected in perfect likeness only with a deeper intensity, the shadows of the woods in all the colors of the rainbow.

Outing to Pine Portage. A.J. McDonald is in the white hat, his wife seated directly in front of him. To the left of Mrs. McDonald is Mae Rooney, and beside her, her brother, Ranger Bill Rooney. **[Bill Rooney Collection]**

Arriving at French Portage, a short walk of a quarter of a mile to French Lake, where another and larger gasoline boat was waiting soon brought us to headquarters where we were warmly welcomed by Mrs. McDonald. Here to our surprise we found all the comforts of a modern house. A well-built log house with logs neatly hewn and the inside covered with beaver board was most homelike and the spacious rooms and office were all spic and span. A furnace in the basement heated the house and a flowing well also in the basement supplied the waterworks, giving everything an air of comfort. Around the house a good sized clearing with a generous stock of vegetables being harvested attested to the care and work of the superintendent. Close by is a substantial log house occupied by a man and his wife as helpers and used by the fire rangers of the park as headquarters when in from their respective stations.

The park, which occupies over 1 1/4 m acres stretches south to the international boundary and from the international boundary line west to Rainy Lake. Here Hunter's Island with its magnificent lakes and rivers and over 9 billion feet of standing pine occupies a large portion. In order to protect this magnificent heritage of timber wealth the department have fire rangers stationed throughout the park year round. At present, there are only 8 outside of the superintendent and his assistant, Mr. Thomas Cooper. Considering that the park covers such a large territory the number of men should be 28 instead of 8 and the wages paid should be increased at least 25 per cent. At present the men are paid $60.00 a month and with this they have to board and clothe themselves. Owing to the scarcity of good men and the high rate of wages being paid elsewhere Superintendent McDonald finds it extremely difficult to get good men. While he does not complain it is nevertheless a fact that the government do not pay enough attention to this important part of their heritage in New Ontario. Because this new park is so far removed from Toronto is no reason why it should not *receive the same consideration as the Algonquin in Old Ontario. When one sees what little means the superintendent has to work with it is hard to believe that so much can be accomplished with so little to do it with. Situated some 11 miles from the railway with two portages over which to haul supplies and the crudest means to do this it is surprising what has been done. Sheltered huts well and substantially built to the number of 13 are now scattered over the park. Here a stove, bed and cooking utensils for the wandering tourist or rangers are placed for their convenience.*

The lakes teem with fish and the woods with game but none may be caught or taken except certain fish and that with a license from the superintendent of the park. As a result of the preservation of the game, moose and deer abound, also wolves and bears in considerable numbers.

On the occasion of our visit we were treated to an 18 mile launch ride across French Lake and down Pickerel Lake to the first shelter hut built on Lookout Island. A side trip to which we were piloted by Mr. Thos. Cooper, the competent assistant to Superintendent McDonald, up the Windigoostigwan river and across the work of the beavers, showed what these pioneer lumbermen were doing. One large beaver dam stretching 50 feet across the river and some 7 feet tall was a truly wonderful spectacle of what the beaver can do in the way of construction. That they possess considerable engineering skill is easily seen when one stands and gazes at the splendid dam erected and so strongly built that it would take a considerable flood to tear it away. Mr. Cooper informed us that there were hundreds of dams and houses along the banks of the rivers and streams. "In fact" said he "they are a great nuisance and cause much damage as a logging outfit". Several trees up to 13" in diameter were seen here and there fallen where they were wanted with others marked for future operations.

One of the most interesting trips was across French Portage to Lake Windigoostigwan a distance of two miles which we took in company with Superintendent McDonald. This is the portage cut out by Dawson and used by the Voyageurs and Wolseley soldiers at the time of the first Riel Rebellion. Here at the end of the portage can be seen the remains of an old dam where the waters were backed up to admit the landing of the large barges with their tons of supplies and army accoutrements. Old iron kettles, broken and thrown aside, bolts, spikes, anchors, and numerous other articles can be picked up almost any place, all marking the spot which was the scene of great activity 50 years ago. The road between the two lakes has been put into good shape by Mr. McDonald so that our trip, which was made with a team and light wagon, was a big improvement over the trail as it was even five years ago.

A favorite route now for American tourists is to come into the park by way of Winton, MN to Basswood Lake, thence north by several routes to French Lake and out to Windigo Station [on the CNR] by way of this long portage and Windigoostigwan Lake. There is no finer outing in all Canada than a trip through this beautiful park reserve. There is still a lot to do and in order to do the work properly the superintendent must have more help. He works himself like a beaver and there is no job he cannot do, whether it is paddling a canoe, travelling on snowshoes or swinging an axe. Mr. McDonald is equally at home. He loves his work and the wild forest life. He is stern in discipline, yet withal kind to his men but he hates a shirker. If any man hires as a ranger and thinks he has only to paddle a canoe and lay up some miles from headquarters putting in time he has another guess coming. It is good, reliable men who will do their duty as well 100 miles away as if under the eye of the superintendent that Mr. McDonald wants.

Mrs. McDonald is also a thorough woodswoman. She can paddle a canoe and handle a rod or gun as good as the average man; while for preparing a meal there is none better in the land. She is most hospitable to strangers and often gives up the bed for some wandering American tourists and takes a shake-down on the floor in order that the tired tourists can enjoy a comfortable bed. Her larder is always well supplied with plain, wholesome food in which delicious preserves from the many wild berries can always be found on the table. Fresh fish forms a staple diet in the absence of fresh meat and it is Mrs. McDonald that knows how to cook them.

Although this large park reserve is the centre almost of the Thunder Bay and Rainy River districts there are very few even of our people who know anything about it. There are also very few of our government officials at Toronto that have any conception as to its size and beauty. This should not be. The people should take more interest in their own and see for themselves what a glorious heritage we of Ontario have in this Quetico Park Reserve.

The hamlet of Kawene was part of Osborne's story, as it was part of many Quetico stories. The hamlet was named in 1912 when the first post office opened. The name "Kawene" is said to mean "No" in Ojibwe.

Kawene was the closest railway point to the park headquarters at French Lake -- even closer when the administration moved to Eva Lake. Many travellers destined for Quetico left the railway at Kawene's little station. As Sylvia Bjorkman wrote in her recent history of the district, "This influx of people kept Kawene busy, as trappers also passed through continually, and prospectors got off the train with their canoes, obtained needed supplies, and paddled into the wilderness." This remained true until passenger traffic on the line ended.

Ranger at Kawene Station in 1913. The station at Kawene provided access to the Quetico headquarters at French Lake. The half-mile road to Eva Lake was very rough. From there, a barge carried horse and supplies to the portage between Eva and French lakes. **[Bill Rooney Collection]**

However, the trip from Kawene down was not a leisurely stroll. In 1916, A.J. McDonald reported, "On account of scarcity of labour last season I had to abandon work on the wagon road from Eva lake to Kawene station, over which we have to haul our feed, provisions and other supplies. I hope next season to be able to put this road in good condition as during the summer it is almost impassable." All communication between the park staff and their superiors in Toronto travelled across that near-impassable trail.

The next season never came for McDonald. In February 1917, he was reassigned to a job with the province's Forestry Branch in North Bay.

Hugh McDonald: 1917-1925

As his successor, A.J. McDonald originally recommended ranger Bill Darby, but McDonald said Darby "was also offered the position as Chief Fire Ranger in Fort Frances and preferred that position as it was not so isolated as Quetico." Instead of Darby, McDonald then recommended his brother Hughie: "He knows the woods well in almost all the Park," A.J. wrote, "having lived in this District for fourteen years past." Hugh McDonald was appointed Superintendent that month.

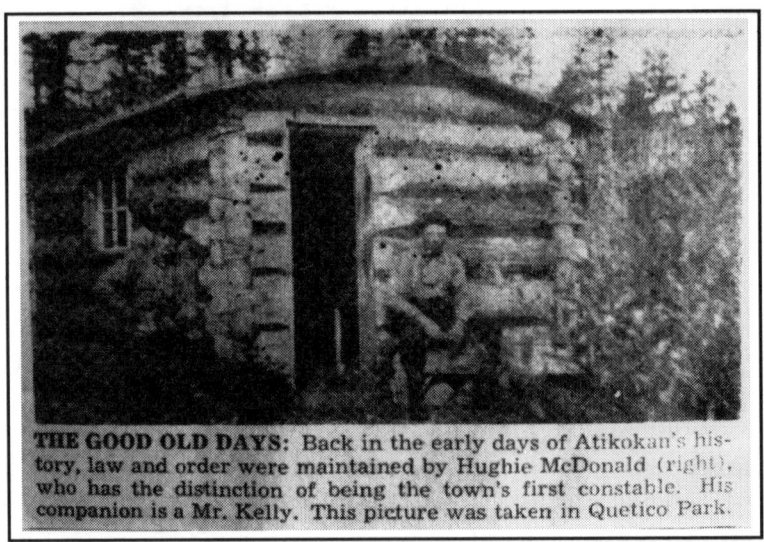

THE GOOD OLD DAYS: Back in the early days of Atikokan's history, law and order were maintained by Hughie McDonald (right), who has the distinction of being the town's first constable. His companion is a Mr. Kelly. This picture was taken in Quetico Park.

[Atikokan Tweedsmuir History]

'Hughie' remains a somewhat shadowy figure to us now. Only one photo of McDonald has been found, showing McDonald seated and smoking a pipe in front of a log cabin. The photo's caption says:

"THE GOOD OLD DAYS: Back in the early days of Atikokan's history, law and order were maintained by Hughie McDonald (right), who has the distinction of being the town's first constable."

McDonald's 'law and order' record was somewhat unusual. Myrtle Rawn Leishman recalled: "Hugh McDonald was the constable in the early days at Atikokan and he found a cache of liquor submerged in the river (during prohibition). He lost his job due to over indulgence as well as exposing himself as the culprit. [He was] a man quite full of fun. Quite a drinking man. I don't think he would have been very capable of doing any book-keeping."

In 1918, he received a letter from the Dominion Commissioner of Customs at Ottawa, informing him that he was being charged with having smuggled goods into Canada. (At the time, there were no customs stations on the U.S. side of Quetico, a serious problem in such a remote area.) A few years later, in 1921, McDonald was again in hot water for having hired three new rangers without departmental approval. Of course, McDonald's superiors in Toronto were 1,000 miles away.

The situation came to a head in late 1924, when McDonald's annual report -- and its deficiencies -- earned him a strong rebuke from the Deputy Minister of Lands and Forests. At issue: the lack of information regarding "the number of fishing licenses that have been issued and their classification...No consideration was given to any revenue that was received for any or all purposes in connection with the Park, nor the number of Guides that were granted licenses with their names."

McDonald resigned his post in 1925, when it was alleged he spent the park's fishing and guiding license revenue -- about $1,200 -- on alcohol.

McDonald's coming (and going) was the first of many changes that overtook Quetico in the late teens and early '20s. During this time, decisions were taken that would have far-reaching consequences for the park and the growing numbers of tourists who enjoyed it.

In 1917, the provincial government created a new Forestry Branch within its Lands and Forests Ministry. This new Branch was charged specifically with fire prevention duties, and a new Forest Fire Prevention Act was brought in to support that role. The scattered handful of fire rangers would finally get some much-needed back up.

Old wooden fire tower at Beaverhouse Lake in 1923. **[Bill Darby Collection]**

Also as part of the fire prevention program, the province directed that the first fire lookout towers be built. For decades to come, these towers would become a familiar sight to anyone travelling in the wilder regions of Ontario, north and south. Quetico's first fire tower -- a 50-foot-high wooden structure -- was built about three-quarters of a mile from the park headquarters at French Lake. The towers were to be connected to the telephone system, eventually, and more than 4 000 pounds of telephone wire was shipped to Kawene for this purpose. Between 1915 and 1925, the so-called "Tree-to-Tree Telephone Line" was built from Kawene to Flanders via Sturgeon, Lonely, Jean, Badwater, and Beaverhouse lakes.

The long-standing complaints of understaffing were also dealt with. In 1917, 33 people -- including 29 rangers, two road-makers, Superintendent McDonald, and the headquarters' housekeeper, Mrs. Fiola -- worked for Quetico Provincial Park. The rangers were paid an additional $50 per year, bringing their pay to $750 annually. Mrs. Fiola earned $300 for her work at French Lake.

Park Employment -- 1917

A.J. McDonald (Jan.)
Hugh McDonald (Dec.) -- Superintendent (Feb.)
William Darby (Dec.) -- Ranger & Sub Chief (July)
Robert G. Johnston (Dec.) -- Ranger
Harry Mack (Dec.) -- Winton -- Ranger
M. Ryan (March) -- Winton -- Ranger
Thomas (Thos.) Cooper -- Ranger & Sub-Chief (July)
William O. Both -- Ranger
John (Jno.) Kelly -- Ranger
George Dancer -- Ranger
Télésphore Fiola (Dec.) -- Ranger
Mrs. T. Fiola (Dec.) -- Housekeeper
Thomas (Thos.) Brady -- Ranger
Walt Hurn (May) -- Winton -- Ranger
Harry Shields (May) -- Kawene -- Ranger
Gus Norland (Oct.) -- Kawene -- Ranger
A. Young (Oct.) -- Kawene -- Ranger
A. Johnson (Oct.) -- Kawene -- Ranger
A. Chelgrin (Oct.) -- Kawene -- Ranger
Fred Fiola -- Ranger
R. Ferris (Oct.) -- Kawene -- Ranger
Alf Both (May) -- Kawene -- Ranger
Albert Both (May -- Kawene -- Ranger
George Morton (May) -- Kawene -- Ranger
F. Foard (May-quit work Aug. 13) -- Winton

Ulric Brzeau (May) -- Winton -- Ranger

Walt West (May) -- Kawene -- Ranger

J. Powell (May) -- Winton -- Ranger

M. Powell (May) -- Winton -- Ranger

M. Anderson (May) -- Winton -- Ranger

Moses Fontaine (May) -- Winton -- Ranger

Pete Spoon (May) -- Winton -- Ranger

Harry Quinn (Sept) -- Kawene -- Road Makers

John Bergen (Sept) -- Kawene -- Road Makers

How little the international border meant -- Winton, of course, was on the U.S. side.

Tragically, the staff were affected by the worldwide influenza outbreak of 1918-19. Millions around the world died of the infection and millions more were stricken. In January 1919, ranger Harry Mack -- stationed at Cabin 16 -- contracted the flu and died. Earlier, he had been helping look after the Powell family on Saganagons Lake, as they, too, had contracted the infection. A doctor came out to Cabin 16 from Ely, but Mack could not be saved. Hugh McDonald reported that the Mack family were "in financial difficulty," so the province paid for Mack's funeral in Winton.

Wilderness Voices: The Powell Family

The Powell Family are inextricably linked to the story of Quetico Provincial Park. From their homestead at the head of Saganagons Lake -- now within the boundary of the park -- members of the Powell family lived off the land, trapping, hunting, fishing, and farming.

Mrs. Jack Powell. Her maiden name was Ottertail. Frank remembered how tame the caribou were and how his mother felt sad to shoot them. ***[Powell Collection]***

The Ojibwe people had used Saganagons for centuries. In 1857, H.Y. Hind wrote that, "The Little Seiganagah [sic] is a favourite wintering place of numerous families of Indians, it abounds in fish and near its shores the winter road to Fort William runs." (Frank Powell later commented that Saganagons is a garbled version of the Ojibwe name, "Kaw-gog-ah-min-e-sains-e-gok," meaning, "A group of islands all attached together down the middle -- like beads strung together.")

Jack Powell and his wife, Mary Ottertail (Okgua-wi-ash-eke) of Lac La Croix, moved to Saganagons in the early 1900s. Together, they raised their children -- sons Bill, Mike and Frank, and daughters Esther and Tempest. Jack taught the children to read and write, while Mary taught the traditional skills of her people. Tempest recalled travelling with her mother to Lac La Croix once, where Mary's half-brother was the chief. It is said she was a fine hunter.

Jack Powell and daughter Tempest with wolf pups. **[Powell Collection]**

The Powells began working in Quetico early in the park's history. Jack and son Mike -- then only 15 years of age -- served as fire rangers in the early 1920s, carrying out patrols from the cabin and old wooden fire tower at Kawnipi Lake. Frank Powell also learned to fly...Frank said he watched the loons landing, and just followed their example! Bill later opened a resort on Saganaga, where Tempest Powell and her husband -- Irv Benson -- settled after World War Two. They met while working as fishing guides in 1946.

Tempest and Irv carried on the Powell family traditions, living at a cabin about 12 kilometres from the end of the Gunflint Trail. (The

The Powell Family taking winter supplies in canoes from Winton and Prairie Portage to their home on Saganagons. **[Ben Ambrose Collection]**

Frank Powell's "Standard" aircraft at the homestead on Saganagons. **[Powell collection]**

trail was named for the Gunflint formation rock found there.) They made a living from trapping and guiding, using dogsleds for travel until snowmobiles came into fashion. It was said Tempest could snowshoe for hours, longer than most of the park rangers.

Tempest Powell Benson on the trapline in the 1950s. The sleigh is piled with beaver pelts. ***[Powell Collection]***

Irv Benson breaking his way through the ice with a boat on Saganagons Lake in November. ***[Powell Collection]***

Mike Powell taking the bull (cow) from Winton to the Saganagons homestead by canoe. [Powell Collection]

Here is one of many stories involving the Powells -- The Canoe Country Cow, as told to me by Bill Magie:

> *About July 1927, I was headed through Ottertrack (Lake) with Walter Anthony. I said, "What the hell is that comin' down the lake? Let's go look." So, we went over there to the far west end. It was Jack Powell, and his sons Frank and Mike. They had a cow on a scow! The scow was about 8 feet long; they had a canoe and a motor on each side of it. They had a halter on her, and her hind end was tied to both corners, so she wouldn't tip the whole works over. They were comin' up the lake! I said, "Where the hell you goin' with this?" (I knew Jack Powell real well.)*
>
> *"Well, you know we been eatin' dried milk for years, but we never get no fresh milk." I'd seen 'em that year, cuttin' all the wild hay they could find. There was two or three big haystacks by their place on the east end of Saganagons. They had four hundred-pound sacks of oats, too, in the scow with the cow.*

When they'd get to a portage, they'd put a horse collar with a couple tumplines over the cow. They'd hook it up to the scow, and the cow would drag the scow over while they portaged the canoes and motors. So, I said, "Hell, we're gonna turn around -- we gotta see that!" They were gonna go through Jasper and come out in Saganagons.

So, we went back with them to that portage. They hooked the cow up, and she hauled the boat up over the hill and down. We helped carry some of their packsacks across.

They got the cow home all right. I saw it about two weeks later. They had a barn already built for it. They were feedin' it wild hay and oats, but they finally had to shoot the cow that winter. She couldn't survive on that wild hay -- got too skinny. So, old Jack shot the cow and they ate it.

Jack told me later, he says, "Bill, it didn't survive on that wild hay. We got wild hay from Kawnipi, Saganagons, and Northern Light. We cut it in the meadows with hand scythes, and hauled it home."

Well, it didn't work out. They went back to dehydrated milk after that. But, I'll never forget seein' that thing come down the lake!

Nineteen nineteen was a bad year for fires -- the fire crews were kept busy with 22 blazes in 21 days (29 May-18 June 1919). The fires consumed 15 000 acres of forest, damaging parts of three timber berths in or near Quetico.

McDonald reported on the many challenges in his first year as superintendent:

"About May 1st we cut a telephone line from Kawene to headquarters, but owing to lack of material as well as

the dry season we did not put in the line until later. The line is about twelve miles long, running south from Kawene to the southwesterly corner of Eva lake, thence east to French lake...I had a saddle trail cut along the line which will be convenient in repairing the line as well as in getting out to the station [at Kawene] in the spring and fall seasons when the water and winter routes are closed. Shelter huts were erected on Kinippi [Kawnipi] lake, and on Lake La Croix this season. Owing to a heavy hail storm in August the roofs on huts on Eden Island, east arm of Quetico and Burntside lake were destroyed, but have since been repaired. Small additions for cooking purposes have been added to the huts on Beaver House lake and Darby's island on Basswood lake.

Kawnipi Lake cabin built in 1916. **[Bill Darby Collection]**

"*Owing to the exceptionally low water this season many new portages had to be cut on the main canoe routes and when not otherwise engaged the rangers are employed cutting inland trails. I regret to say we had considerable forest fire on the south-west end of the Park which destroyed some timber, all of which I understand will be cut this season thus less-ening the loss. Considering the exceptionally dry spring season and the forest fires all around us at that time, I consider that we were very fortunate on the whole. Lumbering operations are very brisk on the south-west end of the Park, but are carefully watched by rangers. ...Game and fur are increasing rapidly, particularly moose, red deer and beaver. Partridges are also becoming more numerous. The weather during the present month has been the roughest I ever experienced at this time of year, causing great difficulty in getting in supplies."*

*Men going in single file toward the kitchen building for Sunday noon dinner. [**Rudy Hink Collection**]*

It was at this time, near the end of the War, that intensive logging began in Quetico. In 1918, more than four million board feet of pine was cut from Timber Berth 51 on Quetico Lake, Timber Berth 38 on Beaverhouse Lake, and W13 south of Anne (now called Kasakokwog) Lake. The next year, Shevlin-Clarke cut a further 26 million board feet of pine from three more berths. The company was operating five lumber camps at Quetico and Beaverhouse lakes. Even the timber rights to Lac La Croix First Nation went on the auction block.

Loading Crew with Hubert Pearson on the left, at Shevlin-Clarke Co. Camp Number Seven in the Namakan River area. **[Hubert Pearson Collection]**

The expansion of Shevlin-Clarke's interests in the Park touched off one of the greatest political scandals in Ontario history. The crux of the scandal is well summarized by Gerald Killan in *Protected Places*:

> *"In 1917...Howard Ferguson, then lands and forests minister, abused his discretionary power to dispense with statutory regulations regarding tender and public competition and sold a timber limit in the park to the Shevlin-Clarke Lumber Company of Fort Frances. The license set dues well below the prevailing rate. James A. Mathieu, Conservative MLA for Rainy River, happened to be general manager of the company. ...Two months prior to the provincial election of 30 October 1919, Ferguson had granted, without public competi-*

tion, a license to the Shevlin-Clarke Company to cut in timber berths 45 and 49 (Near Quetico, Boulder, and Red Pine Lakes) in Quetico Provincial Park, an area of about 5,400 hectares. James A. Mathieu himself admitted that he had set the dues of $9.50 per thousand board feet when the going rate was closer to $20."

The government stated the 1919 tenders were $10 below the prevailing rate because Shevlin-Clarke was conducting a slash burning experiment.

Many voters would not have it, and a huge Shevlin-Clarke investment in victory bonds did not sway public opinion. As historian Peter Oliver wrote, J.A. Mathieu was one of "a new breed. They practiced their trade with a reckless abandon that ignored the regulations of governments on those few occasions that they were unable to strike a bargain with the politicians."

Albert Cain, J.A. Mathieu and son Tommy looking over logging operations.

The controversy over this issue helped defeat the Conservative government in the 1919 provincial election. (J.A. Mathieu was narrowly returned in Rainy River.) The new, fire-breathing Farmer-

Labour administration pursued the scandal with vigor. The Timber Commission was appointed to investigate all charges. Despite damning testimony from many people involved in the government's Forestry Branch, Ferguson survived the scandal, became Conservative leader and won the next provincial election.

Logging continued in the park, though Mathieu soon departed Shevlin-Clarke. He struck out on his own, purchasing the Border Lumber Co. Eventually, he replaced Shevlin-Clarke as the main licensee in Quetico -- by 1954, his companies had processed 800 million board feet of lumber. However, Mathieu was less lucky in politics than in business -- the Labour Party defeated him in 1923. Clearly, some local opinion remained on the side of the companies and their Conservative allies, as this newspaper editorial from the *Fort Frances Times* in 1920 demonstrates:

> *"The great country between the head of the lakes and Manitoba was little more than a howling wilderness but a decade and a half ago up to 1904...then a change was wrought. Such captains of industry as T.H. Shevlin and E.W. Backus came and saw and invested. Last week Judges of the Supreme Court W.R. Riddell and F.R. Latchford came to 'investigate' the lumbering operations of Shevlin-Clarke (a concern which has been perhaps the great single factor in the progress of Rainy River District during the past 10 years). Young men were browbeaten in an effort to make them convict themselves."*

The same paper trumpeted in 1923:

> *"The great white way has been transferred from Broadway to Quetico Forest Reserve. The Shevlin Clarke Company have just completed installation of two up to date electric plants at their camps. Camp[s] 1 and*

2 have been the fortunate ones to have these modern features placed in the bush. A.F. Scott, Supervisory Electrician for Pioneer Builders Ltd. has just returned after turning on the juice much to the delight of the men. Reading lights have not as yet been installed at head of each bed, but at that, the improvement is rather conspicuous. The equipment is a one and a half kilowatt Fairbanks Morse plant with storage batteries. The charging is done by a gasoline engine. This is just another improvement inaugurated by this Company to improve the conditions for their men in the woods."

Thomas Henry Shevlin, Minneapolis, President of the Shevlin Carpenter Lumber Co. [**Minnesota Historical Society**]

In contrast, a Fort William paper, the *Bulletin*, remarked bitterly that "Attorney-General Mr. [W.E.] Raney has dropped his suit against

Shevlin-Clarke Company in regard to cancellation of license on two timber berths in Quetico Forest Reserve. And so fades a big part of the millions of dollars that were going to be recovered from the timber robbers of Northern Ontario."

The Shevlin-Clarke Mill at Fort Frances.

Two sawing crews for Camp Three, Red Pine Lake. **[Rudy Hink Collection]**

The business of running the park went on. Cabin 16 and Cabin 11, both on the south side of the Park, were now manned year-round to control access by American tourists. Then, as now, the Park was much closer to the burgeoning population of the American Mid-west than to Southern Ontario, over a thousand kilometres away. By 1920, Minnesota and Wisconsin -- the two states nearest Quetico -- had a combined population of about five million people. The whole of Ontario then counted fewer than three million people.

Tourist on the dock in front of Cabin 16, Basswood Lake. **[Bob Halliday Collection]**

Hugh McDonald recommended that tourists be offered "every inducement" to enter the park from the Canadian side -- entering from the park's upper side, the tourists would purchase provisions from Canadian businesses and hire Canadian outfitters. This was not happening because "the Canadian National Railway through trains were not scheduled to stop at Kawene, the chief point of entrance on this side."

Quetico's two-man ranger patrols now covered about 250 square miles each, using the park's growing network of ranger cabins. Men like Jeff Seeley, Tom Quinn, Walt Hurn and Ted Dettbarn paddled and snowshoed the trails of Quetico. Cabin 11 became particularly well known for Walt Hurn's garden -- one American visitor boasted that "the rhubarb leaves were as big as umbrellas."

Walt Hurn's noted garden at King Point Cabin 11, Basswood Lake, in the 1920s. **[Bob Halliday Collection]**

The rangers watched for poachers in the winter, fought fires in the summer, and cleared portages in spring and fall. However, some of the park duties were more unusual, as told in this account from September 1921:

Wild Animals Captured by Superintendent of Quetico Park

To capture alive and ship to Toronto a live deer, a porcupine and a beaver on seven days' notice is some feat even for an experienced woodsman. This is what was accomplished by Mr. H. McDonald, the Superintendent of Quetico Forest Reserve [sic]. The Ontario Government wished to secure some representative specimens for Toronto Exhibition and probably without any idea of the magnitude of the task gave Mr. McDonald only seven days to gather a collection. Although real-izing that the time was far from sufficient to get much of an exhibit, Mr. McDonald and his assistants went to work. A beaver was asked for, so a trap was set near a beaver dam. To prevent a beaver from liberating himself from a trap the trapper must either make his set so as to drown the beaver or else use a spring pole to hoist him clear out of the water. A continuous watch had to be kept on the trap so as to liberate the captive and avoid injury. One A.M., while leaving the set to obtain break-fast two deer were observed out on a point jutting out into the lake. Mr. McDonald sent his assistant to play dog and drive the deer into the water, while he in the canoe kept them from swimming ashore. After getting the deer in the water the other had to walk a mile to get a rope and another canoe. Mr. McDonald alone in his canoe paddled alongside the buck and grabbed him by the horn in such a way as to keep the deer from using his feet as a pile driver. There followed some interesting moments. A deer, unlike a moose, is a perfect demon in the water and in the fierce struggle he managed to swing the canoe across his back and swamped the canoe. However, the doe was captured and although fighting her captivity, was successfully crated and expressed east. While the struggle with the deer was on, Mr. Beaver took the opportunity to investigate the trap. When the men returned a full grown specimen was hanging in the air by one leg. In the struggle incident to his capture the leg of the beaver was broken. Dr. William Thompson of Chicago, who is camping close to the reserve, was communicated with by tele-phone. He agreed to come over and offer his profes-sional services. An anesthetic was administered and the broken leg amputated above the break and the skin properly sewn. Within an hour of the operation, the beaver was contentedly munching on poplar bark.

That fall, the Farmer-Labour government tightened its hold on the reigns of power by appointing a new deputy minister -- Walter Cain -- in the Lands and Forests Department. Cain would remain in his post for 20 years, exerting a great deal of influence over park policy. Almost immediately, he announced that "It is not the wish of the Department to do any trapping in the Quetico Reserve this year." Beavers in Quetico had been trapped in previous years to bring in extra revenue.

Another critical change came to Quetico when the first bush planes took to the skies. It was a revolution. Travel was compressed from days of canoeing and portaging to hours of take-off and touch-down. The Ontario government pressed planes into service almost immediately: in 1921, the first aerial surveys of Northwestern Ontario were conducted, creating a true record of the area's forest resources and geography for the first time.

Planes also went into the fire patrol business, as the *Fort William Bulletin* reported in August 1921:

> *"One of the Dominion Forestry Branch inspec-*
> *tors in reporting his first week's experience from an*
> *airplane, records the fact that men camping in the*
> *woods or out from the city for a few days are suddenly*
> *and effectively reminded of what they ought to do by the*
> *appearance of an airplane high above them, attending*
> *strictly to its business of patrolling the forest. This*
> *impression deepened when the men realize that they and*
> *their camp have been seen from the airplane. Of this*
> *they are certain when they see a message fluttering*
> *down to them through the air...They find a message*
> *reminding them that as citizens of Canada, they should*
> *assist the Forestry branch and air board in protecting*
> *their own property -- the forest -- by being careful with*
> *fire. As preventing fires is more economical and effec-*
> *tive than fighting fires, this feature of airplane patrol is*
> *of great importance."*

J.C. Dillon writes that the first aerial forest fire report was made that same month -- August 1921 -- when a plane on a mapping mission discovered a fire at Cliff Lake, north of Quibell.

In 1924, the Ontario Provincial Air Service had been founded, and in April that year, the Service began hiring pilots. The Service used the town of Sioux Lookout -- northwest of Quetico -- as a western base of operations.

It was a dangerous business, as was reported in August 1924:

"...[T]he ill-fated forest patrol plane G-CAOC was seen to slip into the air above Lac des Mille Lacs, near Savanne station by two fire rangers, late on Saturday afternoon, and nose dive to the ground near the lake...The two men hurried to the scene of the wreck where they found Junior Pilot Kenneth McBride dead in the tangled mass of wreckage while Forest Observer Victor Gilbert was terribly injured but still breathing and Senior Pilot E.C. Burton was badly hurt but not fatally. Gilbert died before the airmen reached Port Arthur by the Canadian-Pacific No. 8 train.

It was stated that another plane G-CAOB in charge of Pilot 'Duke' Schiller had left Sioux Lookout on a sketching cruise and had not returned, so Burton was instructed to patrol the district towards Savanne to search for him. Savanne is a fuel station for the air service and they were about to land and refuel when the crash occurred."

By 1927, a temporary air base had been established at Eva Lake, at the site of what's now Quetico Centre. One of the first planes used by the Air Service there was the Curtiss HS-2L "flying boat," which became a common sight in the North in the 1920s. Ted Burton, the son of E.C. (Ed) Burton, said the Ojibwe people called his mother 'sposh a ka ninny weewan,' the 'flying canoe man's wife.'

G-CAOC crashed in the bush. **[Tom Woodside Collection]**

Another long-time HS-2L pilot, Tom Woodside, was honored with a lake name in Quetico -- Woodside Lake lies just west of Agnes Lake in the park's interior.

The "flying boats" proved to be slow and limited in their capabilities, so the Air Service moved to replace them with the DH-60 Moth. Though not without its faults, the Moth was a simpler and more reliable aircraft, and many of them remained in service until well after the Second World War. The Moths logged thousands of hours on patrols across Northern Ontario.

Of course, the planes were put to other uses. One American pilot, C.R. "Dusty" Rhodes, went into the poaching business along the border. Professor Julius Wolff of the University of Minnesota, Duluth, wrote:

"On Dec. 3, 1930, [Dusty] and a trapper were surprised on a lake in Cook County [Minnesota] by wardens Berglund and Hackey. The two got away but the plane was identified. Once he '...is said to have bombed the game warden headquarters in winter with skinned beaver carcasses.'"

Tom Woodside, pilot, standing on HS-2L. **[Tom Woodside Collection]**

The "flying fur poacher" was eventually nabbed on the Canadian side at Lac La Croix and arrested. The RCMP set up a stakeout for him on Lac La Croix, and when he landed, two officers paddled out to his plane. Rhodes fled, and took off with one Mountie clinging to the pontoons. Rhodes landed again immediately, but only after one of the Mounties smashed the cockpit window and put a gun to his head. Rhodes was fined, and took off for parts unknown. His employer -- a mining company in Minnesota -- was left to extricate the impounded plane from RCMP hands.

One of Dusty's acquaintances would become one of the Boundary Waters' best-known characters: Benny Ambrose.

*Dusty Rhodes and Leo Chosa standing beside the plane. Dusty Rhodes was suspected of picking up poachers with their furs. **[Bob Halliday Collection]***

Wilderness Voices: Benny Ambrose

Benny Ambrose was never sure of his age, as births were not registered in Amona, Iowa until 1911. His father was born in Iowa of English stock and his mother was from Germany's Bavaria. After his mother died when he was eight, Benny lived with his stepmother until he was 12.

For much of his early life, Ambrose was a prospector. Even as a young boy, he loved rocks and could always be found down by the river looking at water-washed stones. One of his uncles showed him how to use dynamite, a skill he would use many times in the future.

One of Benny's uncles also caught 'gold fever,' went prospecting in the southwestern United States and disappeared.

Ben Ambrose with beaver pelts. [Ben Ambrose Collection]

Having served overseas in World War One, Benny decided to renounce 'civilization.' Having heard stories about northeastern Minnesota from an Ojibwe man he met overseas, Benny arrived at Grand Portage in the fall of 1919. He then made his way to a cabin on McFarlane Lake, where he spent the winter trapping.

In June of 1927, Benny moved to Ottertrack Lake, where his wife Val eventually joined him. Benny chose Ottertrack because he thought he was close to the legendary gold of Chief Blackstone. He never did find it! The story lived on.

For the remainder of his long life, Benny lived and worked in the boundary country, prospecting, trapping and collecting the most incredible collection of tall stories ever heard. Eventually, he and

Dorothy Molter -- another long-time resident -- were made U.S. Forest Service volunteers, so they could continue to live in the Superior National Forest.

Benny was witness to many important events in Quetico's history: for example, he guided Senators Shipsted and Nolan when they came to investigate Edward Backus' dam proposals. A friend said that Benny was "infinitely superior, skillful, a crack shot, the finest of company, an A-1 cook, clean, does not drink nor smoke," and, of equal importance, "catches fisher alive for zoos, runs them down in three or four days time in winter."

Another friend, Roy Watson, said at Benny's memorial service that, "He was a teacher to young and old alike; a story teller who loved to laugh, and he laughed loudest and longest when the story was on him. He was a strong man, a man who somehow survived a thousand calamities."

The rock cairn in memory of Ben Ambrose at his homestead, on the American side of Ottertrack Lake.

When Ambrose died in 1982, Shan Walshe remarked: "I have always admired Benny Ambrose as the epitome of the pioneer spirit. Over-civilized individuals who have lost this spirit would condemn him as eccentric, foolhardy, anti-social, irrational, or just plain crazy. On the contrary, he was wise, self-reliant, brave, strong both in mind and body, and most of all he was kind. Not for Benny a city job with its prosperity, security and comforts. He preferred to eke out a living with pick and shovel and sleep in a tent at 40 below zero. To the end Benny stood on his own two feet, propped up by no one. Would that more of us had that same proud spirit!"

*CF-OAH Hamilton aircraft picking up telephone line crew on Jean Lake, December 1932. **[Oscar Frederickson Collection]***

On the ground, communication was revolutionized by the construction of telephone lines. In 1924, the *Ely Miner* reported that fire rangers in Quetico were building a telephone line from Agnes lake to Prairie Portage -- there, the line would tie in with the Minnesota State Forest Service line from Prairie Portage to Fernberg Lookout. A United States Forest Service telephone line connected Fernberg Lookout to Ely. So, by calling out via Ely to Fort Frances, fires could now be reported immediately in the southern part of the park.

One change which did *not* come to pass was the creation of an International Peace Park embracing Quetico-Superior. Support grew for a park dedicated to all the men killed during the War. J.A. Mathieu

-- temporarily out of the Provincial Legislature, but still very much involved in the lumbering business at Quetico -- was not supportive. Writing to William Finlayson, then Lands and Forests Minister, Mathieu stated: "Just off hand, I can't see any particular benefit in making a treaty between U.S.A. and Canada, which would create an International Park."

Mathieu added: "I can see a good deal of benefit in having a close co-operation between the Minnesota authorities and the Ontario authorities...There is at present good feeling and co-operation in that respect which I think could be widened..."

While the Peace Park did not materialize here, close co-operation between Americans and Canadians helped derail a plan that could have seriously threatened Quetico-Superior: the water power scheme of Edward Backus.

Backus

Edward Wellington Backus was a businessman. He was also, in the words of Peter Oliver, "a swashbuckling Minneapolis promoter," and "a hard-driving ruthless entrepreneur." Backus was a true Timber Baron, owning enormous (and lucrative) timber and pulp limits along the Lake of the Woods and the Boundary Waters.

He also owned water power rights in the same territory, and therein lay his plan: Backus intended to harness the hydroelectric potential of the Boundary Waters. Control dams would be established along the many lakes and rivers of the region, permanently altering the landscape. "If completed," writes Gerald Killan, "the dams would raise water levels in the border lakes by at least 4.6 metres and as much as 24 metres, with incalculable damage to the scenic and recreational qualities of the area."

This wasn't the first time the issue of water power had come up. Many smaller-scale dams had already been constructed -- for example, back in 1872, a dam was constructed at Pickerel Lake by the Dominion Government to facilitate travel on the Dawson Trail. By 1927,

Shevlin-Clarke had rebuilt that dam to sluice logs into the Quetico River. In 1914, Backus himself built a control dam at Kettle Falls, and all the logs floated out of Quetico had to go through there.

However, nothing like Backus' audacious, sweeping proposal had been seen before, and it ran into stormy weather almost immediately. Conservationists, various levels of government, local communities, and other businesses raised strong objections to the plan. In 1925, the issue was referred to the International Joint Commission, set up by the U.S. and Canada to help resolve disputes over cross-border water issues.

Shevlin-Clarke Pickerel Lake Dam. Simon Dawson built the first dam in 1872. Shevlin-Clarke rebuilt the dam in order to sluice logs through Batchewaung Bay to McAlpine Lake and the Quetico River System. **[Bob Halliday Collection]**

This referral -- the so-called "Rainy Lake Reference" -- was scrupulously investigated by the IJC. The Commission spent almost five years just charting the Boundary Waters, to determine what the effects of the Backus dams would be.

Four main groups opposed Backus: companies that held water rights on the Winnipeg River, which would be affected by the change - their claim was that no additional power generation was required;

communities along the Boundary Waters; the Minnesota State government; and the conservation movement. The Quetico-Superior region was already on the conservation radar: a long fight to expand wilderness protection in Minnesota paid dividends in 1926, when additional protection was won for three large areas in Superior National Forest.

Ernest Oberholtzer, now living at his retreat on Rainy Lake, spearheaded the anti-Backus campaign. With the help of many allies, Oberholtzer fashioned an alternative proposal for use of the Boundary Waters. The plan accepted logging in the region, but argued for strict protection of many parts of the watershed, especially shoreline allowances. A treaty between Canada and the U.S. would seal the deal and provide for joint management in the future.

In January 1928, Oberholtzer and other American conservationists formed the Quetico-Superior Council, both as a vehicle for promoting this alternative, and preserving the Rainy Lake area. The Council hoped to win the co-operation of the Ontario government in this battle -- the Conservative administration of Howard Ferguson was not interested. The idea of an international treaty removing provincial control over Quetico would never gain provincial acceptance (though the Council kept the flickering treaty flame alive for almost 30 years). Little public sympathy was roused for the cause in Ontario: as would always be the case, the main centres of population in the province were a vast distance away, and those centres were generally unaware of Quetico's existence. The large American population close to Quetico-Superior was more aware, and more interested, in preserving this corner of the wilderness. This reality would affect conservation efforts in Quetico many times in the future.

The Council battled on, and scored a huge victory in 1930, when the American Congress passed a bill (the *Shipstead-Nolan Act*) severely restricting water power developments along the Boundary Waters. By this point, the Great Depression was battering North America so badly that logging was dropping to a standstill. The Department of Lands and Forests reported that "during the winter of 1931 there were practically no logging operations in the Rainy River

District." Backus' hundred-million-dollar business interests were about to collapse -- his company went into receivership.

Conservation efforts on the American side gained further momentum in June 1934, when President Franklin Delano Roosevelt created a "President's Committee for the Quetico-Superior" to support the preservation of the area. Among supporters of the Quetico-Superior movement were Arthur Hawkes; Jules F. Prud'homme, the city solicitor for Winnipeg; John W. Dafoe, the editor of the *Winnipeg Free Press*; and H.H. Richards, manager of the Royal Bank in Fort William.

Finally, in 1934, the International Joint Commission ruled that the Backus plan could not proceed. Lawrence Burpee, the secretary of the Canadian section of the IJC, wrote of the Boundary Waters: "...the territory tributary thereto is of matchless scenic beauty and inestimable value from the recreational and tourist viewpoint -- nothing should mar the beauty of this last great wilderness."

Backus did not long outlive his plan. He died of a heart attack in November 1934.

"King John of the Quetico" -- John Jamieson, 1925-1935

During the early stages of the Backus fight, John Jamieson replaced Hugh McDonald as Quetico superintendent. Jamieson had worked as a timber cruiser and scaler -- he was also a friend of J.A. Mathieu. Jamieson earned the nickname "King John of the Quetico" for his sometimes-imperious style.

However, even this King had a superior. Walter Cain, far away in Toronto, lost no time in imposing his stamp on park operations. Cain's lengthy, detailed letters began piling up on Jamieson's desk. For example, this early missive from September 1925:

> *"Regarding the portages and trails, particularly those that are necessary to be used by the rangers, I have to direct you to require the rangers to cut out these trails just as soon as the tourist season is over, before the*

snow comes. You will allot to each ranger the number of trails he is to clear and have him report to you when this work has been done. After it is done, you will take the first opportunity of inspecting it in order that you may see they are properly cleared out...The ordinary portages between the lakes which are used by the tourists and others should be indicated in some way on the shore. A blaze on a tree is not very lasting nor very prominent. A small board sharpened like an arrow and nailed on a tree would be better, or if you consider a waxed pasteboard sign tacked on a board and nailed to a tree would be better, will you kindly notify the Department when a small supply will be furnished."

John and Veronica Jamieson on their wedding day.

Cain demanded that "illegal hunting or trapping in the Park must be stopped," and he suggested "heavy fines or imprisonment in case the fine cannot be paid, would appear to be the most effective and confiscation of all firearms etc., should be made in every case."

Suppressing trapping was not that easy. In early 1926, Jamieson was forced to telegram the RCMP in Fort Frances requesting help controlling poachers in the McKenzie Lake area. Jamieson wrote: "Outlaws trapping on park through information one stated that they will not be taken without shooting require help."

As for Jamieson's request to allow gill-netting of fish in Jean Lake, Cain wrote frostily: "The issuing of licenses to fish in a provincial park for commercial purposes is a very doubtful proposition especially in a small body of water where they could be exterminated." No gillnetting took place in Jean Lake.

"Two aces:" Rangers Ted Dettbarn and Tom Quinn in front of Cabin 11, King Point, Basswood Lake. **[Bob Halliday Collection]**

However, Toronto thought it appropriate to ship ring-necked pheasant eggs from Rondeau Provincial Park to Quetico as part of a 'beautification program.' Pheasants are not native to the Rainy River District.

Other, more productive work was accomplished under Jamieson's supervision. Jamieson himself had a reputation for strictness: his nephew, Gerald Crawley, recalled that "I liked [ranger] Tom Quinn, he was more of an uncle to me than my own uncle because Jamie was so gall-darned strict, you had to do just exactly what he wanted you to do."

To inspect the south side of Quetico, Jamieson took the CN train to Fort Frances, another train to Virginia, Minnesota, and another to Ely. When he arrived, word was quietly sent out to warn the Canadian rangers. He went by car to Winton, and then took a boat to the four-mile portage, where rangers would meet him.

In the summer of 1926, a new wooden fire tower was installed at Lac La Croix. Three Norway pines were used as the base, while guy lines had to be canoed in to complete the tower. On a clear day, it was said you could see 30 miles from the top of that tower.

More survey work was completed to help the fledgling Air Service. Lands and Forests reported: "Important survey lines were run and ground control established by Ontario in the Quetico Park regions...under the direction of the Survey Branch this ground work will, it is expected, be utilized the coming flying season by the Dominion engineers in extending their aerial photography and direct mapping of countless lakes and other information for the service of the public."

Not all the missions ended in success. The Chief Forester at Fort Frances, George Delahey, was nearly killed in 1931 when his DH-60 Gypsy Moth went down over Rainy Lake. Tragically, the crew sent to find Delahey (Nip Greer, Vic Stewart, Phil Hutton, and A.J. Runciman) were killed when their Hamilton crashed during the search in the same area. Delahey survived and lived to a hale old age before dying in 1981.

Crash of Hamilton aircraft CF-OAI at Rainy Lake, August 1931.

George Delahey's DH-60 Gypsy Moth. The plane overturned on landing in windy conditions on Rainy Lake in 1931. **[George Delahey Collection]**

Rangers Walt Hurn on the left from Cabin 11, and Ted Dettbarn from Cabin 16 on Basswood Lake. The two men are shown here at Fall Lake. **[Bob Halliday Collection]**

On the ground, the rangers -- many of them now veterans of Quetico's backwoods -- continued their work. Sig Olson, the renowned American conservationist, described one of those great veterans in *Listening Point*:

> *"The scraggly little pine on the end of the point belongs to the memory of Walt Hurn. It is bent and twisted, had once been flattened against the rock by some storm on the past, only to point upward again. ...Walt Hurn, once Canadian ranger at King's Point just to the north, was like that pine, for he too had weathered the storms and in the process had become just as gnarled, indestructible and indigenous. Al-though it has been thirty years since I checked in with him on my way to Quetico Provincial Park as a young guide, I can still see the great spare shoulders bent desperately over a report, the rootlike fingers moving slowly across the page with a tiny stub of a pencil all but lost between them, fingers used to rocks and boulders, to ax work and the heavy*

packs of portages. During those days he was King's Point, part of the log ranger station nestled under the tall Norways, part of the brooding cliffs of Ranger's Bay behind and the broad sweep of water toward Jackfish and the outlet. The fluttering Union Jack was more than a symbol of authority in an outpost of the Empire. To me it meant Walt Hurn."

Another ranger, Bob Wells from New Brunswick, later recalled that all the rangers had to spend a two-week session working the garden at Park Headquarters. He remembered the rangers were even required to pay 10 cents per pound for potatoes out of the garden, "after us planting them and hoeing them and everything!"

Bob Wells on the right with John Sansted at Cabin 16, Basswood Lake. **[Bob Wells Collection]**

Many years later, Wells recalled that he first came to the park in April 1927. Then working as a logger for Shevlin-Clarke, he had heard Quetico was in need of rangers. So, he and another logger, Borden Parker, went to the French Lake Headquarters looking for work. They got it. The two greenhorns were sent to a cabin on Pickerel Lake, where they were to patrol for poachers all winter. The two didn't take enough provisions and nearly starved in the spring of '28, waiting for the ice to go out.

Wells had many adventures before he left Quetico in 1941. He said he recalled seeing wigwams along the Wawiag, and remembered the infamous squatter of Fred Lake, Jim Gannon. Of him, Shan Walshe wrote: "Very little was known about this recluse except [stories] that he possessed a large number of guns...and was wanted by the law." In the 1930s, Wells said thousands of deer flourished in Quetico, but moose were scarce, owing to the "blind staggers" disease transmitted from deer to moose.

*Bob Wells on the left, with Jess Valley on Basswood Lake in the 1930s, testing the ice with a canoe between them. **[Bob Wells Collection]***

One of Wells' colleagues, Ted Dettbarn, wrote this report about tracking down more poachers in 1928. (The text has been edited.)

The 8th we travelled across country headed for Cabin 18. When we struck Louisa Lake, we saw a man's track...we followed him up to Fauquier Lake where we found 8 traps set for beaver. We broke them up, but could not locate the men, as the ground was bare in lots of places then. We will go back when we have more grub with us and try to find them...there is another party somewhere towards the Shade Lake route. We saw some tracks on one place leading that way. Tom ran across 2 big Finns...coming in...at Meadow Lake and turned them back. As he was alone at the time, he did not take their outfit, as they were dangerous looking fellows. One had a long Colt Revolver (8-inch barrel) hanging around his neck by a string. Ole Harris and his partner Sansted are out somewhere, too, and there may be more we don't know about from Ely. Tom thinks we should have more help here at the present time. The airplane whizzed by again right after we got here, flying about 30 feet above the ice. We could not see him very far this time -- don't know where he went. We will pull for Agnes Lake Monday and look over the Shade Lake Route and around Fauquier Lake, then cross over to Carp Lake. If the going is too poor, we can make it by land over there. It looks now as if it will be a late spring.

About the time Wells became a ranger, Jamieson hired one of the park's earliest female employees: Miss Noreen Miller. Miller wasn't a ranger -- she worked as a teacher for Jamieson's two children, Agnes and Mac. However, Jamieson had hired Miller without Walter Cain's approval. When Cain received the bill for Miller's wages, he was furious. He wrote: "This is the first intimation the Dept.

has had of a school being in operation at Park Headquarters or, in fact, at any point in the Park." Eventually, the bill was paid.

Jamieson's wife, Veronica, was also on staff, officially holding the position of housekeeper at Park Headquarters.

In 1928, John Linklater, a well-respected Minnesota Game Warden, guided a group on a trip from Basswood Lake along the border to Lac La Croix. The purpose of the trip was to publicize the fact that women went on canoe trips -- several women, including Vi Sansted of Winton, Minnesota, accompanied Linklater on the journey. Apparently, photographers recorded the trip, as photos of Sansted were displayed at the World's Fair in Chicago in 1929!

Left to right: Andy Matchette, Mrs. Jamieson, Kelly, Mac and Agnes Jamieson, Ranger Albert (Frenchy) Lemay, and Miss Noreen Miller. **[Gerald Crawley Collection]**

*Vi Sansted camping on Lac La Croix. **[Sansted Collection]***

The Boundary Debate

Among Ontario provincial parks, Quetico is unusual in that its boundaries have been increased -- and reduced -- on many occasions. (Algonquin Provincial Park, for example, has never been reduced in area, only increased.) However, since the original Quetico Forest Reserve was established, the biggest single change to the park boundaries occurred in May 1931. At the urging of John Jamieson, the government extended the park north to include all the territory between the existing park boundary and the Canadian National Railway line. On the west, the new line ran south along "the present travelled road from Flanders Station to Beaverhouse Lake." In so doing, the government protected more than 1,600 square kilometres of land and several major lakes -- including Eva, Nym, Crystal, and parts of Windigoostigwan.

The purpose of the change was simple. Poachers in the northern areas of the park could simply travel overland to the railway line, hop a train, and disappear, never to be caught by park rangers (or the RCMP). By extending the park all the way to the Canadian National, rangers could track their quarry right to, and on, the railway. According to the Order-in-Council making the change, the government stated that the Order created "a fixed boundary line which is difficult to do with the present boundary as it runs through several Lakes and Rivers." In addition, the Governor-in-Council stated that "within this area there is no large quantity of commercial timber."

There was a major problem with this boundary change. The area added to the park included several hundred residents and parts of the communities of Abiwin, Kawene, Sapawe, Atikokan, Banning, and Flanders -- all railway villages straddling the Canadian National. Dozens of cabins and other buildings were spread across the area.

Reaction from some quarters was swift. Having become the Conservative MLA for Rainy River once again, J.A. Mathieu forcefully opposed the plan. In June 1928, when the change was still under consideration, he wrote:

> *"There are quite a number of buildings south of the Canadian National Railway on the area you suggest adding to the Park; some of them are squatters, there are some trappers and some hunters also have buildings on this land. Before this land is added to the Park it would be only right and fair to go over this territory and ascertain how many people are living on it; I am quite satisfied it will be a hardship to quite a number of people to be forced to move off this land.*
>
> *I might say that in general the public are not much in favor of adding anything more to the Quetico Park they rather feel that there is a large enough percentage of this district already in Parks."*

In another missive, Mathieu added:

> *"Quetico Park is really a game reserve and not much of anything else. I venture to suggest, however, that there are other portions of the District in which game is very much more plentiful than in the Quetico Park reserve and there is much better fishing in portions other than Quetico, notwithstanding the fact that game has been protected in this park for about twenty years. I believe this is the only park in North Western Ontario notwithstanding the fact that the District of Rainy River is rather a small area compared with other Districts in that portion of the Province and I am very much opposed to the placing of any more of the lands in the District into parks."*

Remarkably, the government ignored the advice of its own local MLA and expanded the park.

Deputy Minister Walter Cain heard the protests even in Toronto. Shortly after the boundary extension, he reported to John Jamieson that "There have been objections raised to the extension of the Northern boundary of the Park, one sent in by Mr. Cullen on behalf of the Atikokan Angling Association and the other in the form of a petition." Cain made the extraordinary request that Jamieson "investigate the petitioners claims with regard to occupation. ...The Department is also anxious to ascertain the citizenship of many of these parties whose names are foreign, and it is for this reason that the list is sent to you." Jamieson was required to investigate 178 petitioners, including 69 employees of the CNR.

The province tried to make the boundary extension more acceptable by waving the fishing and hunting regulations in the expansion area. "But, of course," Cain wrote, "trappers are taboo." The regulations were enforced by (among others) patrols from Cabin 26 at Windigoostigwan Lake, the southwestern part of which had just become park territory.

110

However, extending the boundaries of Lac La Croix First Nation was not so well received by the government. The issue came up when two Lac La Croix men -- John and Edward Tatice -- were arrested for violating park regulations. The Indian Agent at Fort Frances took up the case with his superiors:

"...Owing to the Indians of this Reserve being so badly hemmed in on all sides, I would very strongly recommend that the department take it up with the Provincial Government, and try and get that portion of the lake south of this reserve given to this band for trapping and fishing, as there are very few islands in that portion of the lake, the boundary could follow the Namikan [sic] River to the north boundary of the reserve then turn east and follow the north boundary along the reserve, and then south till it would reach the U.S. Boundary, that would give the Indians a small chance to live up there.

I have just had two of the Indians of this reserve up for being on the Quetico Game Reserve, and the Indians have just reported to me that they were only about one hundred feet from the shore opposite the Lac la Croix Reserve, on the ice, and picked up for being on the Quetico Park, now it is a shame if we allow these Indians to be picked up as soon as they step off the shore, and go on the lake, as all the Indians want to fish and go boating on this lake, and if they are denied this privilege, why they might just as well be in jail."

No change was made to the Lac La Croix boundaries.

The park extension did not withstand the political heat put to it. Thinking perhaps of an imminent election campaign, Premier George Henry eventually moved to undo the boundary changes in 1934. The limits of the park were returned to their original position. This caused still further confusion on the ground: in October of that year, Jamieson reported that a trapper from Owakonze, Robert Sawdo, wished to trap near the park. Sawdo came to the park office to inquire just where the north boundary of the park now lay. Jamieson wrote: "He is going to trap the north shore of Pickerel and from the tracing of the map which you outlined for him and your letter to him there is nothing I can do at the present to stop him."

Henry's staff were no longer present to receive this note, as the Henry government was swept from office in June 1934. Replacing Henry was Liberal Mitch Hepburn, the province's first Liberal premier in almost 30 years. While Walter Cain survived the change of government, many others did not, including "King John of the Quetico." As Jamieson's replacement, Lloyd Rawn, said: "I came in in 1935 and I came in as a result of political patronage. They let a fellow by the name of Jamieson go."

Lloyd Rawn: 1935-1948

Rawn family at homestead on southeast arm of Steep Rock Lake in 1916. [Myrtle Leishman Collection]

112

*Lloyd Rawn, Superintendent of Quetico Park, 1935-1948. **[Bea Rawn Collection]***

Tom Rawn and his wife were among the first settlers of Atikokan in 1899. Soon after, Atikokan was made a divisional point on the Canadian Northern Railway, and the town began to grow. Tom's nephew, Phillip, Lloyd's father, homesteaded on the southeast arm of Steep Rock Lake for a couple of years.

Lloyd was actually born in Marinette, Wisconsin in 1910. His family moved back to Atikokan the following year. Lloyd attended school in Atikokan and Port Arthur, and worked at a series of jobs before his appointment as Superintendent. Park Ranger Art Madsen recalled: "Lloyd Rawn was a political appointment in 1935. He was new to the job but he learned fast and we soon had better equipment and better things for the cabins."

Park rangers in January 1936 at French Lake. Left to right: Tom Quinn, Art Madsen, Bob Halliday, Lloyd Rawn, Bill Croome, Elmer Melin, Dick Madsen (rear), and Albert (Frenchy) Lemay. **[Bob Halliday Collection]**

George Delahey on the left beside a "Moth" of the Ontario Provincial Air Service.

Rawn arrived in the midst of major changes to his park -- the new Hepburn government was rapidly making its mark on the Lands and Forests Department. Large numbers of fire and forest rangers were

114

dismissed and replaced. By March 1935, the division between Fire Rangers and Forest Rangers disappeared as the two forces were merged. The entire park was moved under the jurisdiction of George Delahey, the district forester at Fort Frances. Delahey reported directly to the durable Walter Cain. Art Madsen said: "Geo. Delahey became district forester for the Fort Frances area. Being a world war pilot he flew the plane and got around and saw how awful some of our cabins were. He had good cabins built at Beaverhouse and Basswood, and Bob Halliday, Albert Lemay and I built a nice log cabin at Cache Bay in 1938."

*Left to right: The three sourdoughs -- tough shape: Art Madsen, Albert (Frenchy) Lemay and Bob Halliday at the original cabin on the west side of Cache Bay. [**Bob Halliday Collection**]*

As a means of combating the unemployment of the Depression, a Dominion-Provincial Youth Training Program was launched. A group of boys were brought to Quetico to work. Based at an old boys' camp at Eva Lake, near Park Headquarters, the group worked to clear the route of the park phone line between Kawene Station, Eva Lake and Beaverhouse Lake. This was the first major repair work ever undertaken to the critical lines.

In total, there were 14 boys aged 16 or 17 employed in the work, most of them having come from Rainy River or Fort Frances. At times, they slept on the ground with wool blankets for bedding. A cook, with a portable stove, provided meals. On one occasion, the boys were caught in a blizzard at Badwater Lake, and took refuge in a cabin there. As they watched the snow swirl, there was a scuffle under the floor, and the odor of skunk seeped in. So, the boys had to choose to brave the blizzard, or live with the stink! (Out they went.)

It was an adventure for these boys. The next year -- 1936 -- the young men had no such fun: they were pressed into service during the terrible fire season of 1936.

Boys from the Dominion Provincial Youth Training Program at camp on Badwater Lake standing with the camp cook playing a guitar. **[Gerry Payne Collection]**

Ed Domanski remembered the summer of '36. Ed was in high school when the big fires started in 1936. Because there were not enough fire rangers, they took kids out of the Rainy River schools in June. He recalls:

We flew up to Quetico with a pilot from one of the Winnipeg airways about the middle of June -- right to

[Kawnipi] Lake. He made three trips bringing in 28 fire recruits and 12 fire rangers. We were south and east of Rose Island on the mainland about a mile away. We saw the old fire tower on Rose Island and could see either high hills or trees on the shore beyond. We went in there several times to put out fires. At the time, fire was burning on the southwest part of Rose Island.

We were there on [Kawnipi] for two and a half months with fire all around us, but none where our camp was. That fire must have started toward the end of May. We never had one rainy day. It did rain one afternoon. We came back and our whole tent was blown about 100 yards in the bush. It was hot. We never had a cold day while we were there.

We fought fires in McVicar Bay and Murdock. Sometimes we were taken by motor [7 1/2 hp Johnson on an 18-square-foot stern canoe], but many times we had to paddle. Sometimes we would paddle for three hours before we would come to the fire. I was with the small crews: one ranger and three fire fighters. We had Wajacks [canvas bags filled with water] and a shovel.

On Rose Island, we'd see the fires at night and we'd sometimes walk three-quarters of a mile [at night] to try to put them out. There would be two crews of us -- two rangers and seven or eight men. We did a lot of digging to try and confine the fires.

I was with the Quetico ranger, Alvin Lindgren. [Lindgren later died at the Darky Lake ranger cabin in 1941.] Alvin was Swedish, I think. He was slightly crippled and walked with a limp. He weighed about 135 pounds, but he was very, very strong. He was a most knowledgeable man and I really liked working with him. This particular time, we were somewhere around Murdock Lake putting out small spots around trees.

There was a crew of about eight or nine of us. I seemed to be the only one paying attention. All of a sudden I could hear something like a train. I said: 'Alvin, are we close to the CN over here?' He said: 'No,' and he listened and he said: 'That's a tree top fire, we've got to get out of here and fast.' ...He hollered to the other fellows: 'Drop everything and run to the lake.' Alvin could not run so I stayed back with him.

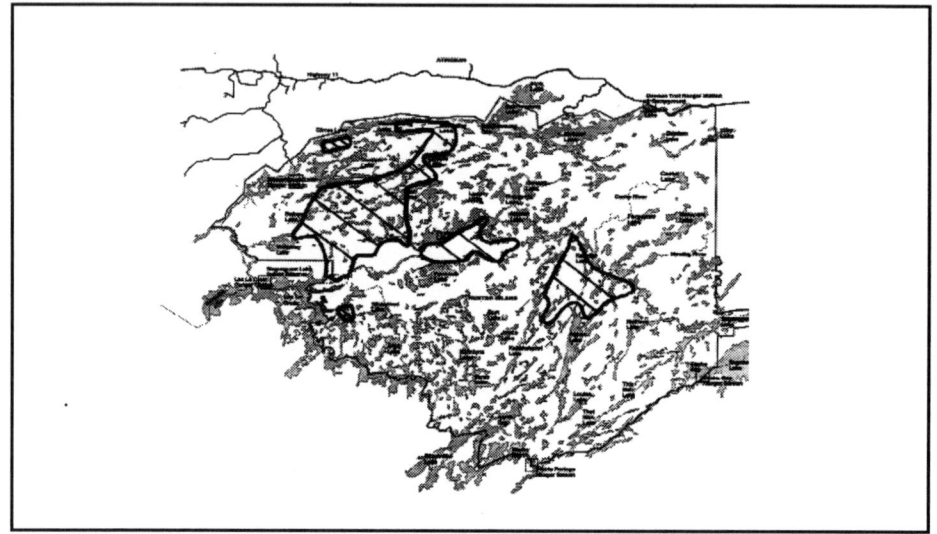

The 1936 fires.

I could have beaten them all because I was a good runner in those days, but Alvin and I ran together with the others about 50 yards ahead of us. We came to a spot about 200 yards from the lake, and the fire was burning overhead in the white pine trees. Branches were falling down on top of us and there was smoke everywhere. Alvin and I ran through half that distance underneath a blanket of fire and got to the boats. It was a hard run, and for him it was terrible -- because he was a lot older. We lost 3,000 feet of hose. We lost all kinds of Wajacks. I remember carrying my shovel, but he said:

118

'Drop it.' But I never thought of dropping it. I remember carrying it in and he said: 'Well at least we've got a shovel left.'

The 1936 fires consumed more than 76 800 hectares of forest in Quetico, marking one of the worst fire seasons ever recorded in the park. Most of central North America suffered under extremely dry conditions. The situation became so dire in August that Peter Heenan - the Lands and Forests Minister, and MLA for Kenora District -- ordered Quetico Park closed to all tourist traffic. No one could enter the park without a special permit from Forestry Officials. By 05 August, Lloyd Rawn noted in his diary that, "Fires are spreading quite rapidly and are entirely out of control. Visibility too poor for flying."

*Logs being hauled on an endless chain from Trail Lake to March Lake by the J.A. Mathieu Company in 1936. **[Howarth Collection]***

*Crew standing in front of a sleigh loaded high with logs. [**Lou Barker Collection**]*

*Endless chain up in the air between March and Trail lakes. This was the longest endless chain ever used in logging and the only one in the Rainy River District. [**Horace Bowes Collection**]*

120

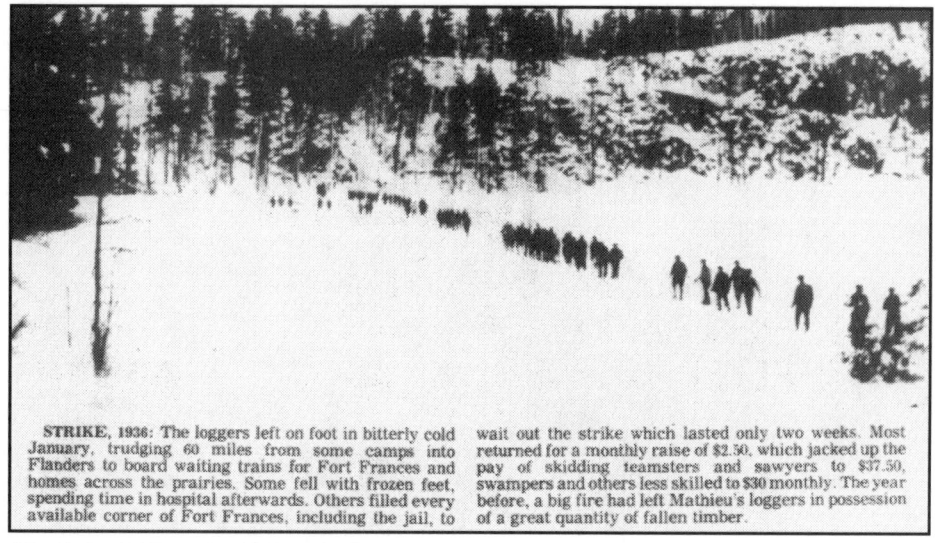

STRIKE, 1936: The loggers left on foot in bitterly cold January, trudging 60 miles from some camps into Flanders to board waiting trains for Fort Frances and homes across the prairies. Some fell with frozen feet, spending time in hospital afterwards. Others filled every available corner of Fort Frances, including the jail, to wait out the strike which lasted only two weeks. Most returned for a monthly raise of $2.50, which jacked up the pay of skidding teamsters and sawyers to $37.50, swampers and others less skilled to $30 monthly. The year before, a big fire had left Mathieu's loggers in possession of a great quantity of fallen timber.

[Ralph O'Donnell Collection]

Eventually, the fires were brought under control. (They brought one small compensation: an extraordinary blueberry crop. Ranger Bob Halliday said he never forgot the sight of them around Kawnipi Lake.) The masses of scorched timber provided a boon for local logging companies. The winter of 1936-37 saw the largest cut of red and white pine in the park's history -- almost 50 million board feet. This was the last large-scale logging of pine in Quetico. About that time, J.A. Mathieu had complained that his 1,000 camp workers were soon going to be out of work, as there was only one more year of profitable cutting left in the entire Namakan River watershed. Mathieu and other northern timber barons also absorbed a pay increase demanded (and won) during the 1936 loggers' strike.

The logging practices of Mathieu and Shevlin-Clarke were criticized by the Izaak Walton League, who said "The Company in its former cutting has stripped the timber right to the water's edge and has made no effort whatever to preserve the now priceless recreational value of the region." A few years later, Mathieu's complaints of a lumber shortage rang hollow when more than 8 000 Mathieu Company logs were wrecked in a jam at Chatterton Falls. Ernest Oberholtzer commented: "Thousand of logs wasted at Mathieu operations at Chatterton and these were among the last available and hundreds of

121

years of growth was wasted...Logging...is the most wasteful imaginable and has created an almost unprecedented fire hazard...especially where the timber was heavy and Caterpillars were used -- huge waste."

*Four-horse team pulling a sleigh loaded with logs during the winter of 1935-36. [**Rudy Hink Collection**]*

*Eight thousand logs of white and red pine wasted in a log jam at Chatterton Falls. The logs were pushed through all at once, so they jammed. The company never bothered to come for them, said Ranger Bob Halliday. [**Oberholtzer Collection**]*

122

Deer behind the office at Orion Lake logging camp #44 in 1937.
[Lloyd Rawn Collection]

The boys of the Youth Training Program were also brought back to work, as the forest fires had badly damaged the Eva-to-Beaverhouse telephone line. The park staff busied themselves with many other repairs and construction projects, including the demolition of Cabin 3 at Eden Island, and the construction of Cabin 36 at Tilly Lake. The old cabin at Cache Bay was last used in 1937 by Art Madsen, Albert Lemay and Bob Halliday, the rangers sent to build a new station at Cache Bay's southeastern point. The first all-metal aircraft of the Provincial Air Service, the Hamilton H-47, was used to bring in lumber. The red pine were cut nearby by the rangers. The District Forester himself, George Delahey, piloted the plane. Several of the Cache Bay staff were befriended by Russell and Eve Blankenburg, pioneers of the Gunflint Trail in Minnesota. The rangers' pay was sent to the Blankenburgs, where the rangers went to visit and pick up their pay.

Cabin 16, on the southern boundary, soon had a new resident: Kay Valley, wife of the local ranger, Jess Valley. A native of Ely, Kay had taken trips with Jess, and was quite familiar with life in the bush. However, initially, the park administration would not give permission for Kay to move in. So, for a time, she lived in a cabin on the American side of Basswood Lake. Jess had a bell installed at Cabin 16 so customers could summon him back from Kay's cabin! In 1938, Kay was allowed to move across Basswood to live with her husband. That same year, Jess oversaw the construction of the 'new' Cabin 16. Kay managed Campbell's Store, a small trading post on the same island as Cabin 16. (The park cancelled the permit for the store in 1955.)

*Art Madsen at Cabin 36, Tilly Lake. **[Jess Valley Collection]***

*Heavy snowfall on the ranger cabin at McKenzie Lake. **[Art Madsen Collection]***

124

*Art Madsen, Bob Halliday and Albert (Frenchy) Lemay building the second Cache Bay cabin. It was a very exposed location for aircraft landings, so the next cabin was built on an island. **[Lloyd Rawn Collection]***

*Cache Bay cabin on the southeast point of Cache Bay. The cabin was constructed in 1938. **[Lloyd Rawn Collection]***

Lloyd Rawn and pilot beside Hamilton aircraft CF-OAH. ***[Lloyd Rawn Collection]***

Russell and Eve Blankenburg were early pioneers on the Gunflint Trail near Saganaga Lake.

The newlyweds, Jess and Kay Valley, at old Cabin 16, Basswood Lake.
[Jess Valley Collection]

The old trading post of Ralph Campbell on Cabin 16 island.
[Gerry Payne Collection]

*Young camper Robert Hattery with George Buckingham, Chief Fire Ranger at the Sturgeon Lake ranger station in 1938. [**Robert Hattery Collection**]*

Family life was also complicated for Bea and Lloyd Rawn. When Bea and Lloyd's first baby was due, they had to get Bea to the hospital at Fort William. To do this, they had to cross French Lake by boat, then walk over the portage to Eva Lake, then cross over Eva Lake by boat, then take a truck from Eva Lake up to the station at Kawene, then take the train to Fort William. Mrs. Rawn was safely delivered of her baby! Tom Quinn, an old ranger by then, called the baby "the *prrrride* of Quetico" in his Irish brogue.

The War Years

The long shadow of another war loomed in 1939. On August 25th -- just days before war was declared -- Lloyd Rawn wrote in his diary: "Left Wet Lake and proceeded through to Headquarters, anxious about the war news -- a very long day. " As German stormtroopers were bombarding Poland, a terrible storm swept over Basswood Lake, nearly ending the lives of three campers. Rawn writes:

128

"Miraculous escape in a storm that swept over Basswood Lake Saturday evening. Mr. & Mrs. Moore and their five-month-old daughter, Ruth, were camped near the Quetico Ranger Station at Bayley Bay when three trees blew across their tent, pinning the family underneath. They were extricated by Canadian rangers. Mrs. Moore received spinal injuries and Mr. Moore was somewhat injured. Baby Ruth was sleeping in a steel crib which saved her from being crushed."

Warehouse at Bayley Bay with roof torn off by storm. **[Bob Hayes Collection]**

Soon, many of Rainy River's young men would be leaving the bush to combat the other storm. One of the first to go was George Delahey, the District Forester at Fort Frances.

The war brought many changes to Quetico, not the least of which was allowing prospecting inside the park. This seems antithetical to the whole purpose of a park, but the wartime demand for resources overrode conservation. No mining ever took place in Quetico -- mining and prospecting were finally banned in 1956 -- but there was

129

prospecting along the Man chain of lakes. In the early '50s, core samples were taken on the north side of That Man Lake (see color insert).

Seven pines fell on the Bayley Bay Cabin from the storm. **[Bob Hayes Collection]**

Lloyd Rawn on the left and Bob Halliday at a portage on the Maligne River on an inspection canoe trip in 1941. **[Bob Halliday Collection]**

The redoubtable Walter Cain retired in May 1941, and was replaced by Frank MacDougall, the former superintendent of Algonquin Provincial Park. A native of Carleton Place and a long-time bush pilot, MacDougall brought actual forestry training to his post. He was the first Deputy Minister to have such experience. MacDougall had left a firm stamp on Algonquin, having worked to curb cottage development and maintain as much wilderness as possible for recreational users. From now on, logging would be seated second to tourism.

Park rangers on patrol in January 1941 at Mosquito Point, Pickerel Lake. Left to right: Bert Sleeman, George Cullen and Bob Halliday. **[Bob Halliday Collection]**

He applied these ideas to the entire park system, and made huge waves. In October 1941, after only a few months in office, he ordered that a uniform uncut area must be left around all park waterways by logging companies. (The allowance was to be 300 feet, or 91 metres, wide.) Such reserves had been demanded by conservation groups, who complained about unsightly cutting by James A. Mathieu along Crooked Lake. Wilson Cram of Kenora, a Forestry official himself, remarked to MacDougall that "...from what I have seen, there has not been concerted effort in the District of Rainy River to provide shoreline reservations in timber sales, particularly in Quetico Park."

J.A. Mathieu was livid. He decried the allowances as a "waste" and "unsound forestry policy." But the decision stood: MacDougall and his new boss, Lands and Forests Minister Norman Hipel, demanded 300 feet. Further restrictions were placed on Mathieu after he secured cutting rights along Basswood Lake -- Canadian Point and Norway Point, near Cabin 16, were exempted from Mathieu's license. Allowances along the lake and along portages were to be strictly enforced. Mathieu complied, and Ernest Oberholtzer later commented that the cutting was an improvement over other Mathieu cuts in Quetico.

Public opinion also spoke out against more logging of Quetico. When it was announced that virgin pine would be logged around McNiece Lake and Yum Yum Lake -- in the park's southern interior -- the provincial government received more than 2 000 letters protesting the decision. The cut was forbidden. The days of commercial logging in Quetico were waning fast, and soon would be over. The results of the logging were roundly condemned -- Ontario Forester J.R. Dickson wrote, "For a generation past, great exploiting companies have been permitted to log and devastate that unique and magnificent recreation land in 'forgotten Ontario' lying between Lake Superior and Lake of the Woods. To make an immediate 'killing' they think nothing of creating an everlasting pigsty." Times had changed.

J.M. Whalen, the acting District Forester while George Delahey was overseas, did not like the logging restrictions. He also opposed a moratorium placed on commercial development inside the park. He wrote:

"My opinion is that Quetico Park is of no value what-ever as a recreational area for Canadians since it is not accessible to them. During the past nine years an average of 1,336 Americans visited the Park each year, while only three Canadians visited it each year. ...No

Canadian outfitter, supplier or guide benefits in any
way, as all supplies and services must come from
Minnesota."

Whalen lost his battle. Leases on cabins and commercial resort developments in Quetico were suspended several times before being prohibited altogether. By 1946, only three private leases had been permitted in Quetico anyway, in contrast to the long string of cottages, businesses and resorts along the Minnesota border. Prohibiting more leases prevented American businesses from simply relocating across to Quetico, as concerted efforts were being made to reduce development in the Superior National Forest.

In spite of these challenges, the compromise of Quetico held. In 1943, Lloyd Rawn wrote in defence of his park:

Quetico Provincial Park was established in 1913, it has
been a protected area since that time. Wildlife still
thrives in spite of everything. If this area were thrown
open there is no doubt that it would mean extinction to
several species of fur bearers. Many residents of our
District derive their livelihood indirectly from the Park.
In 1939 our District was practically stripped of all fur
bearing animals and moose, but the war saved the situ-
ation, the District is again well stocked, thanks to
Quetico. What we really need is more areas where game
is really protected. We owe this to the next generation.
Its [sic] their heritage and we have done little to
conserve it. Quetico is ideally located in the roughest
terrain in the area, the land is of no value aside from a
wildlife sanctuary and a recreational area. Its rivers
and lakes form waterways for canoe travel that cannot
be duplicated. Canadians as a whole do not spend holi-
days in wilderness areas, they live too close to them all
the time, but it is there for them if they want it. Quetico

is the last natural resource in this District and there are a few who would like to exploit it, but I'm sure that there are many more that realize its value and can see a little farther ahead. We have nothing in our District that can compare.

French Lake Headquarters, 1913-1943, located at the west end of the historic French Portage. Hewn logs were used for the walls. The roof and floor were metal and there was a full basement. The first occupant was A.J. McDonald and Lloyd Rawn was the final occupant. **[Lloyd Rawn Collection]**

Rawn's responsibilities were expanded when another boundary change was made -- this time without the controversy of the 1931 expansion. In November 1941, Quetico's limits were extended on the northeast side out to Kawene, bringing Nydia Lake and parts of Eva and Windigoostigwan lakes back into the park. J.A. Brodie, the Chief of the Forest Protection Division, wrote: "The Boundary extension will enable Park authorities to extend their facilities and keep a close watch on trapping and fishing and will make available better landing facilities for aircraft within the boundaries of the Park. The chief point of entry to the park is at Kawene on the C.N. Railway, and it will contribute to the effective supervision of the Park to have the Park Headquarters at

134

the chief point of entrance. Since a new headquarters has to be built, it should be built at Eva Lake near Kawene."

The new headquarters was required because the furnace at the old French Lake building had collapsed. Having survived more than two dozen Quetico winters since the days of Colonel Young, the furnace gave up the ghost in 1937. Lloyd Rawn wrote to Walter Cain: "It is only fair that the condition of the building itself be brought to the Departments [sic] attention, the foundation of the building is badly rotted, racking the building to such an extent that doors and windows fit very poorly and have to be [continually adjusted] to the settling of the building."

Iris Fawcett on the step of the cabin built at the French Lake beach in 1942 -- it was for a two-man ranger patrol. It was built of logs, 18' x 22' with an 8' x 18' verandah. It had a brick chimney and cedar post foundation. **[Borden Fawcett Collection]**

As the tide of the war turned in 1944, the long-standing proposal for an International Park in the Quetico-Superior was revived. Again, the suggestion was made that a park dedicated to the memory of war veterans should be created across the Ontario-Minnesota border. Many parties spoke out in favor of the proposal, including the Ontario section of the Royal Canadian Legion. The Ontario government -- now headed by Col. George Drew and his Progressive Conservative Party - followed the lead of his predecessors and rejected the idea. H.W. Crosbie, the Chief of the Lands and Recreational Areas Division, wrote that "...no advantages will be gained by Ontario in creating such a Park but it would be of great benefit to the tourist industry of Minnesota. ...If the wishes of Minnesota are conceded to, we will be handicapped in developing to any great extent the recreational facilities of Quetico for use by Canadians." In 1948, Drew's minister of Lands and Forests, Harold Scott, added: "The United States authorities have a long way to go before conditions on their side will be comparable to those in Quetico Park in Ontario."

Smaller battles were waged, and won. In 1945, Lloyd Rawn reported:

During the spring thaws of 1945, the Cache River in Quetico Provincial Park, swollen by floods and heavy rains rose to about five feet above normal. This brought the water up roughly three feet on the walls of the old log over-night cabin located on the river bank. When rangers Fred Atkins and Gerald Payne called there after the flood, they found that the beaver had tunnelled under the banking and came up inside the cabin. The pole floor was undoubtedly floating, so they pushed this to one end along with the stove and other odds and ends of equipment, and then proceeded to build a beaver-house in the opposite end. The beaver-house was almost completed when evidently the water receded to its normal height. The boys spent half a day hauling out the mud and sticks and getting things back to normal. There will be no wood problem at this cabin for some time.

Ontario Provincial Air Service pilot Louis Poulin (left) with Gypsy Moth and Lloyd Rawn (right) in the winter of 1946-47. **[James Smith Collection]**

Mosquito Point cabin, Pickerel Lake. It was built with upright cedar logs from an abandoned Shevlin-Clarke building in the nearby logging camp -- the camp operated from 1925 to 1927. **[Bob Halliday Collection]**

1947
Bob Hayes & Gerry Payne
Rangers at Mosquito Point
Grub List for Winter

8 Oxydol; 6 bars soap; 12 bars, Lux face soap; 4 cartons matches; 6 dozen sardines; 1 box apples; 25 lbs. Prunes; 20. Pgs. Raisons; 15 lbs. Split peas; 15 lbs. Dried beans; 10 lbs. Salt pork; 2 sides bacon; 2 whole hams; 1 case tomatoes; 1 case peas; 2 cases corn; 1 case string beans; 4 cases milk; 1 case Klik; ½ case eggs; 20 lbs. Cheese; 5 lbs. Macaroni; 5 lbs. Rice; 6 lbs. Cornmeal; 50 lbs. Butter; 10 lbs. Oatmeal; 6 lbs. Salt; 24 lbs. Lard; 15 lbs. Coffee; 10 lbs. Tea; 50 lbs. Flour; 6 cans baking powder; ½ bushel turnips; ½ bushel carrots; 1 bushel onions; 8 bushels spuds; 3 lbs. Pot barley; 2 cans pepper; 2 cans cinnamon; 2 cans nutmeg; 7 cans jam (mixed); 25 lbs. Corn syrup; 6 bran flakes; 6 shredded wheat; 6 corn flakes; 2 cans cocoa; 20 lbs. Brown sugar; 24 rolls toilet paper; 24 royal pudding; 2 cases canned mixed fruit; 12 cans sauerkraut; 12 lbs. Pancake flour; 5 lbs. Cream of wheat; 1 large vinegar; 6 boxes Ritz crackers; 1 balogna.

Interior of Mosquito Point cabin: Gerry Payne and Bob Hayes bought paint themselves and painted the floor. There was $500 for mainte-nance of the entire park. ***[Gerry Payne Collection]***

138

Ranger Bob Hayes tries skis on the snowshoe trail in 1943.
[Bob Hayes Collection]

Poaching continued to be a concern. In the winter of 1946, a hunt ensued for poachers working the March Lake area. A Gypsy Moth over-flying the northwestern part of Quetico discovered sleigh (or toboggan) tracks leading into the park from Flanders. The plane radioed to Gerry Payne and George Walsh -- the rangers at Sturgeon Lake -- who set out in pursuit. They were joined by the two rangers from Beaverhouse Lake, Arne Korpi and Jim Smith. Eventually, the rangers chased the poachers into the Trail Lake area, where they were apprehended at an abandoned Mathieu shanty.

With the war over, new resources were finally made available again. In 1947, the Provincial Air Service ordered 12 Beaver aircraft for patrol duties, and the Beaver soon became one of the best-known aircraft to work the North. Many would claim it was the best bush plane ever built.

Ranger Gerry Payne at Mosquito Point in the winter.
[Frank Dumeney Collection]

The use of planes became a serious issue in the immediate post-war years, as tourists began flying into Superior National Forest in ever greater numbers. By 1948, it was reported that Ely, Minnesota, was the largest float plane base in North America -- a staggering increase in flights. Conservationist Sigurd Olson remarked that, "Honest sweat and hours of toil should be the admission price to wilderness lakes."

The business of tourism had truly taken flight.

*Gerry Payne, Jim Smith and Arne Korpi at Bentpine Cabin 3 on March Lake, 1947. This was an old blacksmith shop from Mathieu operations, renovated by George Walsh for ranger use. Lloyd Rawn supplied tar paper for the roof. [**Bob Halliday Collection**]*

*The first unpainted Beaver aircraft in the District landed at Mosquito Point, 1948-49. [**Lloyd Rawn Collection**]*

The Road to Atikokan

As Ontario was about to enter the prosperous (and conservative) 1950s, it acquired a prosperous, conservative gentleman to lead it: Leslie Frost. An avid outdoorsman himself, Frost recognized the economic potential of tourism, and his government would take huge strides towards harnessing that potential. In his 12 years as Ontario's Premier, Frost expanded the provincial park system, and invested heavily in a network of highways to carry Ontarians to those parks.

Among the hundreds of projects built by the Frost government was the Atikokan Highway, a project that would connect Quetico to the rest of Ontario. For the first time, the isolated park would be open to the automobile, and would be within reach of the car-driving public of Southern Ontario.

The people of Atikokan had demanded the highway. For decades, the community had relied almost solely on the railway -- and the railways were dying fast. Passenger rail traffic would decline dramatically in the next 20 years, until, eventually, the little station at Kawene would be closed. The old trail to Kawene would no longer be Quetico's link to the world. In 1954, the section of the park above the highway would be removed, and the park headquarters relocated from Eva Lake to Nym Lake.

Building the highway was no mean feat. An unidentified man who worked on the highway project recalled:

> *The road construction began on Highway 120 from Atikokan to Thunder Bay. A camp of about 50 men was on the high flats over the French River. They came to Kawene by train and carried their packs along the old trail to French Lake. Men were sent from the employment office and one crew was made up of men from Lithuania or Latvia. Some were doctors and lawyers. It was early March. One of the Park rangers was of Finnish ancestry and he tried to explain to them what*

they had to do. It was too difficult for them and many quit. Other workers were lumberjacks as winter work in the camps had finished. They lived in tents with floors and walls and heavy barrel stoves. They worked summer and winter and in the summer the insects were terrible. On April 2 they had a pile of slash get away and burn all day by the river. They would sometimes hike cross-country to the beach at French Lake.

A group of 44 prisoners from the Lakehead Jail were also brought out to work on the highway project. The prisoners completed the access road into French Lake, and cleared about five acres for a campground.

For the people who worked at the park, the Atikokan Highway changed the character of the park forever. Pilot Borden Fawcett wrote that, "Prior to the Atikokan-Shebandowan highway, we were sort of an isolated group at the Eva Lake Base. When friends or relatives came to visit via CNR and Kawene, the big highlight was to make a portage trip to French Lake."

Now, park users could drive their cars to French Lake instead. When Lands and Forests Minister Clare Mapledoram opened the Atikokan Highway in 1954, he announced that one of the six key Quetico Park policies would be "to provide [access] at French Lake which is a natural gateway to the routes of the park. It is also proposed to establish a modern public camping ground at the end of this road on the shores of French Lake."

However, the highway brought new pressures on the park. The Quetico Committee of the Northwestern Ontario Chamber of Commerce -- including members from Atikokan, Fort Frances, Port Arthur, and Fort William -- called for "exceptional precautions" to protect the park's wildlife, now that the highway was going through. (The committee chairman, Steep Rock Mines president M.S. Fotheringham, also complained the park was "too lightly regarded" in the Atikokan district.)

M.S. (Pop) Fotheringham.

Other means of access to the park were also controlled. By 1955, the federal government restricted landing in Quetico's airspace, and a new order prohibited houseboats along the boundary waters. Despite complaints from outfitters, over-winter boat storage inside Quetico was also banned. On the American side, President Harry Truman banned low-level flights over the roadless areas of Superior National Forest.

One new use was permitted in the park: trapping by the Lac La Croix First Nation. The federal Indian Affairs department successfully lobbied Toronto to open up parts of Quetico -- the areas north and west of Hunter Island -- to traplines. The province permitted traplines to be registered in the northwest end.

The campaign for an international treaty to protect Quetico gained new life in the post-war years. In 1949, future Governor-General Vincent Massey helped found the Canadian Quetico-Superior

Committee, to work for the protection and preservation of the park. Quetico was beginning to receive a glimmer of recognition from the populated South. (By 1954, the Committee transformed itself into the Quetico Foundation, which still works for the preservation of the region today.)

In tandem with its American counterpart, the Canadian Quetico-Superior Committee urged the adoption of a treaty creating an International Peace Memorial Forest in Quetico-Superior. A cross-border committee would oversee the management of the park. Sig Olson described the project in the *Steep Rock Echo*:

> *The Quetico-Superior Project is a conservation plan designed to protect and perpetuate the resources of the area embraced by the Rainy Lake and Pigeon River watersheds. It applies to the region on both sides of the International Border from Lake of the Woods to Lake Superior, approximating some 10M acres or 16,000 sq. miles of forested lake country.*
>
> *The region first came into prominence forty years ago when W.A. Preston, member from Rainy Lake [sic], proposed the est. of a million acres in the south central part of the area as Quetico Provincial Park. Pres. Theodore Roosevelt, recognizing that adjacent and on the American side of the border was a similar beautiful lake country, set aside another million acre tract as the nucleus of the now 4M acre Superior National Forest, the largest in the U.S. From that time on, the entire area of the two watersheds has been known as the Quetico-Superior.*

As it had several times before, the Ontario government refused to consider any such treaty. The province would not surrender control of Quetico to a higher order of government under any circumstances. Frank MacDougall said, "This great natural park will be controlled and

145

operated by the province of Ontario...It will not be an international proposition." Business interests in Northwestern Ontario -- already resentful of the lock Minnesota had on economic activity in Quetico -- rejected the treaty proposal outright. In 1960, an exchange of diplomatic notes indicated an agreement to full collaboration with the U.S. Forest Service in seeking common policies for the Quetico-Superior country.

The Committee then changed its tack. The group abandoned the treaty concept and moved to endorse the Atikokan Highway, something not supported by some American conservationists. The group also spoke out in support of a park policy statement drafted by the Northwestern Ontario Chamber of Commerce. (Not coincidentally, M.S. Fotheringham was a member of both the Chamber and the Committee.) The Chamber's goals were simple: to keep the Park an unspoiled, beautiful area, but also to make it easier for the general public to get into and enjoy it.

The Chamber's suggestions -- proposed by the people of the Rainy River District themselves -- would be adopted by the province.

Bert Parker: 1949-1955

Lloyd Rawn was not at Quetico to witness these battles. In March 1948, he was appointed to a new position as Lands Specialist, and relocated to Fort Frances. Rawn's replacement as superintendent was long-time Quetico ranger Bert Parker.

Bert Parker, Superintendent, 1949-1955. **[Bert Parker Collection]**

Bert was born in Chilliwack, BC, and spent his early years near Campbell River, on Vancouver Island, and then in Red Deer, Alberta. The Parker family eventually moved east to homestead north of Emo.

Bert had a long association with Quetico, stretching back to the late 1920s. He used to tell a story about an early experience as a ranger...each ranger was allowed to shoot one moose or deer for fresh meat while stationed in the interior of the park. As Bert was paddling down a winding creek one time, he spotted a cow moose on the shore.

147

He took a shot, but the moose disappeared. He kept on until he saw another cow moose. Again, he shot, and again, the moose disappeared. Finally, he had another chance and shot again -- finally, success. So he thought. Imagine how he felt when he discovered he had killed *three* moose: the first two had disappeared because they'd fallen down dead!

Shown at French Lake in 1927: Ranger Bert Parker with Mac Jamieson holding the horse, the schoolteacher Miss Noreen Miller, and Agnes Jamieson. Agnes and Mac were children of Superintendent John Jamieson. ***[Bert Parker Collection]***

*Headquarters house at Eva Lake. [**Bert Parker Collection**]*

*Betty Parker beside the Quetico Provincial Park Headquarters sign at Eva Lake in the winter of 1950. [**Bert Parker Collection**]*

Bert Parker at Eva Lake with dog Nibs standing in front of a Lands and Forests truck. **[Bert Parker Collection]**

Betty Parker standing between two Quetico rangers (Fred Atkins on the right) in 1950. **[Bert Parker Collection]**

O N T A R I O

ATIKOKAN   Quetico Park
Headquarters

Highway 11

Nym
Lake

Dawson Trail Ranger Station
& Campground

Batchewaung
Lake

Cirrus Lake   Kasakokwog
Lake   McAlpine
Lake   Batchewaung
Bay   Pickerel
Lake   Baptism
Lake   Tilly
Lake

Quetico
Lake   Oriana
Lake   Cache
Lake

Beaverhouse Lake
Ranger Station   Jean
Lake   Olifaunt
Lake   Cache River

Lonely
Lake   Sturgeon
Lake   Cache River   Ferguson
Lake   McKenzie
Lake

Basspelt
Lake   Russell
Lake

Sturgeon
Lake

Wolseley
Lake   Kawnipi
Lake   Wawlag River

Negueguon Lake
Indian Reserve   Poohbah
Lake

Lac La Croix
Ranger Station

CANADA
USA   Lac La
Croix   HUNTER ISLAND

Wickaleed
Lake   Burt
Lake   McEwen
Lake   Saganagons
Lake

Joyce
Lake   Agnes
Lake   Cache
Bay   Saganaga
Lake

Argo
Lake   McIntyre
Lake   Kahshahpiwi
Lake   Cache Bay
Ranger Station

Sarah
Lake   Thie
Man
Lake

Louisa
Lake   That
Man
Lake

North
Bay

ONTARIO

LAKE OF
THE WOODS   Atikokan

Fort Frances   Bayley
Bay
Thunder Bay

International Falls   Baswood
Lake   Prairie Portage
Ranger Station

SUPERIOR
NATIONAL FOREST

Ely   Virginia

Hibbing   LAKE SUPERIOR

Bemidji

Duluth
Superior

MINNESOTA

WATER

QUETICO PROVINCIAL PARK

ROAD

RANGER STATION

M I N N E S O T A

N

A Paleo-point of Hixton silicified sandstone. Note the fine workmanship with the parallel flaking, which was distinctive for the Paleo-Indian period. This point is approximately 9 000 years old. The point was found by Bob Nault of Atikokan.

Tanner Lake and Rapids, where John Tanner was likely shot.

Fire base at Bayley Bay, Basswood Lake, 1935. One of the best sand beaches in Quetico stretches across the north shore of Bayley Bay. To the left of the fire ranger base is the portage to Burke Lake. **[Gerry Payne Collection]**

Drill cores from That Man Lake.

Mist rising over French Lake.

*Joe Kaliska, who was on patrol with Gerry Payne at Robinson Lake in the winter. [**Gerry Payne Collection**]*

*The Robinson Lake cabin. Gerry Payne and Frank Dumeney stained it. [**Gerry Payne Collection**]*

Cache Bay Ranger Station in the late 1950s. ***[Gerry Payne Collection]***

Jean Goff in the bow with Charlie Ericksen, operators of the Nym Lake Voyageur Wilderness Programme.

"Painted Rock" pictograph cliff site on Lac La Croix.

Shirley Peruniak interviewing Bill Magie at his home in Solon Springs,
Wisconsin, in 1979. His faithful dog Murphy is at her feet.

John Ottertail and Frank Jordan, Jr., standing on a point below Lower Basswood Falls during the 1984 Lac La Croix-Quetico Heritage Canoe Trip.

John Ottertail at a campsite during Heritage Canoe Trip in 1984.

Timber wolf at Beaverhouse Lake. **Photo taken by Jon Nelson in 1976.**

"a-ni-mi-gi-mi-ga" (rainbow or path of the thunder)
"a-ni-mi-gi" (thunder)

Author Sam Cook, Ken Gilbertson (U.S.F.S.), Gord Peters (Superior National Forest Regional Archaeologist), Jeff Larson (U.S.F.S.), and Bridget Walshe on a canoe trip with Shan Walshe from Lac La Croix to Grand Portage in 1984.

Myrtle (Rawn) Leishman, Effie Munn, Bea Rawn (who came to French Lake as Lloyd Rawn's bride in 1937), Anna Rawn, and Alice Rooney visit French Lake in 1984.

Quetico-Superior 75th Anniversary Celebration at Prairie Portage in 1984. Left to right: Ontario Minister of Natural Resources Alan Pope, Minnesota Commissioner of Natural Resources Joe E. Alexander, and Deputy Chief of the U.S. Forest Service Ray Housley.

Shan Walshe in 1979.

Aerial view of Shan Walshe Lake, designated in 1991 in memory of Shan Walshe. Surrounded by red and white pine, the lake demands stamina for the portages that access it. That would have pleased Shan. **[Photo by Shirley Peruniak]**

George Halemba receives 25-year MNR service award from Jay Leather in 1995. George originally started with MNR on fire crew and worked in many positions at Quetico Park, including Dawson Trail Campground Superintendent and finally Seniors Operations Specialist.

Mary (Mrs. Pat) Jourdain in 1981. As a child, she traveled by birch bark canoe, snowshoe and toboggan as her family moved with game and fish populations.

Chuck Miller cooking supper at a campsite on Quetico Lake during the Tall Pines Planting Project, May 1992. Chuck Miller became Assistant Superintendent in 1993 and was later Acting Park Superintendent from 1996 to 1998, while Jay Leather was Acting Zone Manager, Northwest Region, Ontario Parks in Thunder Bay.

Ron Geyshick, Ojibwe healer, took part in Visitor Services programs at Dawson Trail; here he is on the French Portage Trail in 1989.

Quetico Park staff having lunch in 1997 on the beach near the future site of the pow-wow grounds at Lac La Croix First Nation. Left to right: George Halemba, Dave Maynard, Brenda Herbert, Chuck Miller, Jerry Lange.

Pilot Dean Gill and Assistant Superintendent Wayne Bourque at the Lac La Croix Ranger Station in 1990. Wayne was park warden (1978-1981, 1983-1984) and Assistant Superintendent from 1989 to 1993.

Geoff White, portage crew, with the burnt area along the Falls chain shoreline in the background in May 1996. Fort Frances Fire #141 burned through this area in August 1995. [**Photo by Dave Dissette**]

Left to right: Stephen Cole, Jack Matthews, Peter Dalglish, George Fells, Ian McLeod, Lloyd Burridge, Peter Gordon – after a meeting of The Quetico Foundation in Quetico in the 1990s.

Atikokan Beavers visit the Quetico Park Information Pavilion in Sept. 1994 [Photo by Grace Mullner]

Canoeing solo in Quetico.

"A Sense of wonder": looking at the nest hole of a Black-backed Woodpecker.

Frank Dumeney from the Robinson Lake patrol in winter.
[Gerry Payne Collection]

Laundry day at the Agnes Lake cabin -- the cabin was at the north end of the lake. **[Frank Dumeney Collection]**

151

After serving overseas during World War II, Bert attended the ranger school at Dorset, and returned to Quetico. When Lloyd Rawn resigned from the superintendent's post in 1948, Bert became acting superintendent, and eventually full superintendent. In 1949, Bert and his dog, Nibs, moved to the Quetico Park Headquarters at Eva Lake. Soon after, his wife Betty joined him at Eva Lake in the winter of 1950. The couple are remembered for their warm hospitality, especially at Christmastime, when they would invite the rangers who could not get home to celebrate the season.

One of Bert's most hair-raising days took place during that first year. Rangers Gerry Payne and Frank Dumeney were stationed at Mosquito Point, while George Walsh and Jack Hodges were working at Wet Lake. Frank had an attack of acute appendicitis, and radioed Bert for a plane. At almost the same time, George Walsh radioed from Wet Lake to say that Jack Hodges had collapsed on the floor. Bert asked, "Is he dead?" George replied, "Well, he's not breathing."

Pilot Jimmie Burton was sent to pick up Frank. Jimmie then flew to Wet Lake, where George met him at the cabin door, bottle of whiskey in hand. The two passed the bottle back and forth over the dead man while deciding what to do. On the way back to Headquarters, Frank had to sit on the corpse, as space was so cramped in the small plane. Upon landing, Frank was rushed to hospital for an appendectomy.

Burton had another harrowing experience when his plane was forced down over Pickerel Lake, near the park's northern boundary. The plane had been sent out to collect fishing license money from the ranger stations and then deliver some fresh meat to ranger George Walsh. As Burton was attempting to land on Sturgeon Lake, one of the struts on the float was damaged, and he took the plane up again. However, the force of the wind pushed the float up towards the propeller. Jimmie radioed a mayday and landed -- on one float -- at Pickerel. (Also on board were George Hendrickson, Gerry Payne and the district forester, George Delahey.)

Jim Burton with his family in winter at Eva Lake. He was later killed while flying a helicopter in Manitoba.

*Airplane CF-OCX crashed in the water. [**Bert Parker Collection**]*

Park rangers (left to right) Galbraith, Ian Wilson, Art Scheirer, and Pentti Aho at the Beaverhouse Ranger Station in 1949. **[Gerry Payne Collection]**

Sign at the Beaverhouse Ranger Station, 1949-50, made by Jean Owen, a tourist from Milwaukee. **[Pentti Aho Collection]**

The rangers managed to swim to safety, and a second plane was sent out from French Lake to pick up Delahey. However, the plane had no room for more passengers, and it was too late for a second trip, so Payne and Hendrickson camped on the beach and ate George Walsh's steaks! The plane lay ditched at Pickerel for some time, until new floats could be sent out from Sault Ste. Marie. Pentti Aho and Garf Carson had to carry the floats over the portage to French Lake.

*Rangers having their hair cut by a fellow ranger at the Beaverhouse Ranger Station. **[Dick Carnahan Collection]***

Some aspects of the ranger's job was changing with the times. In 1949, helicopters were first used in the park -- planes of all kinds were making the old ranger patrols less important. However, fire patrol duty was the same, dirty, dangerous work. In 1949, when a lightning strike started a fire at Suzanette Lake, rangers Pentti Aho, Arne Korpi, John Rumney, and Bob McCool were sent to put out the blaze. Early in the battle, a blizzard of heavy, wet snow descended on Suzanette,

155

smothering the fire. The rangers then had a different problem: their fire hoses froze and the tents collapsed under the weight of the snow. The men were stuck at Suzanette for three miserable days until they could be rescued.

*Fred Dustak and Gilly Dahlin climbing the McKenzie Lake fire tower during construction in 1950. **[Pentti Aho Collection]***

Ranger Joe Kaliska (see color insert) recalled those days in a 1982 interview:

> *Paddy Ryan sent me on to Eva Lake where I was working under the supervision of Bert Parker. He was the chief ranger at Eva Lake at that time. There were other fellows there, Frank Dumeney, Pentti Aho, Arne Korpi, George Walsh, Richard Wood, and*

Carl Wood, they were all classed as park rangers at that time. Of course their work was varied. They were doing scaling, park patrolling, and fire fighting and we were all more or less jacks of all trades there.

*Tent camp at McKenzie Lake in 1950, during construction of the fire tower. [**Pentti Aho Collection**]*

...Bert Parker sent me to Robinson Lake and this is where I met Gerry Payne. Borden Fawcett, who was a pilot at that time, flew me out to Robinson Lake. During the course of our stay...we were on park patrol and we had something like 350 square miles to patrol in the park. It took in Lac La Croix, Iron Lake, Cabin 16, Prairie Portage, Kawnipi, and all those lakes in that area as well as Kahshahpiwi...

157

Lyle Beninger (left) and Joe Plumridge at a fire on Suzanette Lake.
[Bill Beninger Collection]

Gerry and I were in there until Christmastime and during the two or three months that we were in there park patrolling, we had a few exciting experiences. Of course we first started out patrolling by canoe until the lake started freezing over and of course the ice wasn't thick enough so we had to kind of hole up at Cabin 9 which is at Robinson Lake. We had to sort of wait around there till the ice got thick enough so we could start walking on the ice and we could go on snowshoes. That took about a week, a week and a half. We covered a lot of territory. We were doing beaver census, counting beaver houses and so on. Of course we were patrolling the area for poachers hunting deer in the park and so on. We had in our area about eight cabins where we had food stashed...and it was nothing to see a pot of stew hanging from the ceiling where we would let it freeze and we would carry on to the next cabin and of course when we made our next round we knew there was a pot of stew waiting for us hanging off the ceiling there.

I had one hair-rising experience, one that I'll never forget when Gerry Payne and I were going to...Burt Lake and it had a long island with a cabin right in the middle. And my first time in there I wasn't too sure where the cabin was but Gerry had a bit of an idea and of course when we got to Burt it was in the early part of December...some lakes were frozen, and some weren't. I remember Burt was frozen on the east end and when Gerry and I got there at this end it was getting dark already. So Gerry said we'll walk down the centre of this long island and we're bound to find the cabin. Of course, the bush was very thick and snow was on the ground...The darkness came upon us pretty fast there, so I'm walking along and it's already pitch dark and I couldn't find the cabin from the lake shore there. As I'm walking along...something made me stop and I could hear water washing on the shore.

*Pilot Borden Fawcett on the right with Provincial Air Service Engineer Bert Day at Fort Frances Headquarters, 1951. [**Borden Fawcett Collection**]*

...I stopped and took my packsack off and of course I was on snowshoes. I took my flashlight out and put the light and lo and behold I was only about 25 feet from open water...if I hadn't stopped when I did, I would have [fallen] right into the ice-cold water. So I gently back-tracked and followed the shore and I missed the cabin entirely -- I couldn't see it. It was dark and I was hoping to see a light some place but I couldn't even see that. So I walked right to the north end of Burt Lake [island] and the rocks were very steep down towards the water and this is where I slipped again and I started sliding down the rock towards open water again...somehow I managed to get my hand stuck into a crevice there and I pulled myself back up...stumbling around in the dark I fell into a crevice head first. I managed to get out of there...I was listening to see if I could hear Gerry some place on the island there and pretty soon I hear him pounding his wash tub with this stick, trying to attract my attention. So I followed the sound and here was Gerry standing outside the cabin...of course he was soaking wet already and he was trying to get some of his wet clothes off and I wasn't any better, I was soaking wet myself. It was great to get into that cabin and when I told Gerry what had happened, I think Gerry turned white as a sheet...that's the closest call I ever had in all my travels in Quetico Park.

Another fact of Quetico life was that -- as in the past -- few Canadians made the trek to visit the park. In 1951, the naturalist Fred Bodsworth commented, "Last summer, I travelled in Quetico with three other Canadians: Dr. Carl Atwood of the University of Toronto, John Mitchele, secretary of the Toronto Anglers' and Hunters' Association, and Peter Fessenden. When our guide introduced us to passing canoe parties as Canadians, invariably eyebrows were raised.

We were Canadians on Canadian soil, yet in Quetico we were the foreigners."

The Parkers with baby son Gary at Eva Lake headquarters, September 1952. [Gary Parker Collection]

One famous group that *did* visit Quetico were the "modern-day voyageurs" expeditions, led by Sigurd Olson. Olson -- who celebrated the Quetico-Superior in his book *The Singing Wilderness* -- organized several trips to retrace the route of the Voyageurs along the Boundary Waters. Among the participants were the canoeing expert Eric Morse, Dr. Omond Solandt of the University of Toronto, and journalist Blair Fraser of *Maclean's*. Fraser subsequently wrote an article, "We Went La Verendrye's Way," in which he called Quetico "the wilderness, empty and lovely."

However, very soon, the lovely wilderness would not be so empty.

161

*Gary Parker, son of Bert and Betty Parker, on patrol in Quetico. Gary is now a Conservation Officer. **[Gary Parker Collection]***

Drying out, 1950, with the burn of the 1930s on Long Island in the background. Long Island is between Agnes and Kawnipi lakes. **[Dave Granskou Collection]**

*"How to get through here?" Canoeing in 1950. [**Dave Granskou Collection**]*

*Having a break in Quetico, 1950. [**Dave Granskou Collection**]*

*The Voyageurs, left to right: Omond Solandt, Tony Lovink, Blair Fraser, unidentified. 1954. [**Omond Solandt Collection**]*

*Ranger Gerry Payne sold licenses out of this tent during the year they built Prairie Portage (1955). [**Gerry Payne Collection**]*

164

In 1955, the park rangers went to Leo Chosa's Trading Post, met some girls and decided to have a party at Bayley Bay, Basswood Lake. Norman Martinson, Customs officer, is third from left. Gerry Payne is second from right, seated. **[Gerry Payne Collection]**

Ross Williams (1955-1973)

In the parks service, the late 1950s and early 1960s will be remembered as the era of the great Recreation Boom. In those few years, the number of recreational users visiting provincial parks in Ontario doubled and tripled. At Quetico, the number of visitors grew from two or three thousand per year to more than 84,000 in 1963.

This recreation boom demanded a matching outlay of resources -- and the Frost government delivered. The cabinet created a new Parks Branch. Headed by Ben Greenwood, the Branch dramatically expanded the number of parks available to Ontarians. Within a few years, the parks system grew from just eight (Quetico, Sibley, Lake Superior, Algonquin, Ipperwash, Presqu'ile, Long Point, and Rondeau) to more than 80.

165

Ross Williams, Park Superintendent, 1955-1973.

To manage the tide of visitors to Quetico, the new District Forester of Rainy River, Bill Foster, hired Ross Williams as Superintendent. (Bert Parker was promoted to Assistant Lands Supervisor in Fort Frances.) A native of Fort Frances, "Smoky" Williams had joined the Lands and Forests department in 1946, starting out as the operator of a Fire Tower near Emo. He then spent almost eight years as a fire ranger before receiving his Quetico appointment.

Williams said: "[Foster] had an interview with me and he said, 'Would you be interested in Parks?' I said I didn't know anything about them, but I was willing to try it because it was a step up."

Williams earned a reputation as a strict, stern boss. Shan Walshe wrote that Williams "seldom passed a compliment openly, but rewarded an employee in more subtle ways for a job well done. In fact he performed many kind thoughtful acts which he deliberately concealed. A year after I first met him I was dumbfounded to learn that

166

tough, mean, old Ross Williams had actually made frequent trips over the ice to an island in Nym Lake to visit an ill lady."

Ross Williams (on the left) and Mike O'Brien at Cache Bay in the 1970s.

*Ross Williams with his wife Iona and children Keith, David and Lloyd on the steps of Cabin 16, August 1957. **[Dick Stewart Collection]***

Entrance sign at Dawson Trail Campgrounds in 1957. Alvin Tyrvainen of Finland ON was the creator of the beautiful stonework on the French Lake buildings.

Park administration office and museum at the Dawson Trail Campgrounds in 1959.

Together, Foster and Williams oversaw tremendous changes at Quetico. Williams said: "...When I went up to Eva Lake there was absolutely nothing. We had an office up on the hill and we called it the 'Bum's Rest.' At the bottom there was a kitchen, that's where [George] Walsh and I stayed. The guys stayed in a tent. I converted the old warehouse, in the first winter, into a sleeping place because nobody could sleep in the kitchen and eat there all the time. I got fed up with it. I converted the old garage into a bunkhouse. I was in charge of everything so it didn't make any difference."

Aerial view of Quetico Park headquarters and Lands and Forests Air base at Eva Lake -- 16 August 1955. **[Kidd Collection]**

Almost immediately after his appointment, Williams had to manage the construction of a large number of facilities at the new Dawson Trail Campgrounds, and new entry stations at both Prairie Portage and Cache Bay (see color insert). An older building became the first park museum at French Lake.

Some park facilities were replaced or abandoned. Within a few years, Williams had to order the destruction of 35 aging ranger cabins -- the old cabins had been used and abused by fishing parties. With the growth in air patrols, patrol cabins were less necessary. Among the cabins destroyed were Saganagons Lake, Cache Point, Carp Lake, Wet Lake, Sarah Lake, Burt Lake, Darky River, McAree Lake, Lower Sturgeon Lake, the cabin at the Beaverhouse Lake dam, Oriana Lake, Mosquito Point, Kawnipi Lake, and Agnes Lake. Williams commented sadly: "You used to be able to leave anything and it was respected...The motorboat people left terrible messes on Batchewaung. People came with chainsaws and lawn chairs."

The picnic shelter at French Lake in 1958, soon after its construction.
[Kidd Collection]

Williams commented that "We were a different type of people just after the war...[There was not] just an 'esprit de corps.' We had an interest in our job. ...We worked hard... I remember working on a fire for five days one time. I lost ten pounds. I was small then and I would go night and day."

The original Eva Lake air base, now beyond the park's borders, was closed -- a new base and park headquarters then opened on Nym Lake in 1957. Williams said, "We had the plane year round... For some reason, years ago, they decided that because...we were isolated...and we had people out in the park...the plane was based here.

Before that, there had been a Moth. So when the Beaver came in, it was based at Eva Lake so we could supply our park stations or ranger stations with food, or if there was a poacher or some kind of a contact."

Evelyn and Bob Halliday, U.S. game warden and pilot Bob Hodge and his boss from Minnesota. ***[Gerry Payne Collection]***

The Hallidays left Cabin 16 in January 1957, moving into the partially completed house at French Lake.

At Lac La Croix Ranger Station: Bob Halliday visits Carl Johnson, on right, in 1963. ***[Bob Halliday Collection]***

As long as there were motorboats, there was a lot of garbage.

Nym Lake base under construction. Left to right: Art Colfer (pilot), Bill Foster (District Forester), Joe Kaliska (Fire Centre, back to camera), and Fred Dustak (Fire). **[Lew Ringham Collection]**

Nym Lake Fire Base, early 1960s. **[Adrien Van Rooyen Collection]**

Pickerel Lake Concrete Dam, built 1956-1957. **[Bruce Litteljohn Collection]**

The province also invested $100,000 to replace the dam at Pickerel Lake, raising the water level back to a controlled level.

Gerry O'Reilly sitting on boards on the Kahshahpiwi Tower in the 1960s. **[Adrien Van Rooyen Collection]**

174

The old, wooden fire towers had been replaced by steel towers. In 1963, a steel fire tower at Pal Lake, north of Atikokan, was disassembled and hauled to Kahshahpiwi Lake. A crew of five -- including John Halasz, Gerry O'Reilly, Dwight Robinson, Mike Stus, and Harry Whitehead -- did the work. O'Reilly was offered the job as towerman if he would help reconstruct the tower! He did, but the crew suffered a near-fatal accident when a propane refrigerator malfunctioned. An insect got into the vent of the fridge and blocked it, causing a build-up of carbon monoxide in the cabin. The men had closed up all the cabin windows because of bear problems.

Aerial shot of Kahshahpiwi Fire Tower.

O'Reilly gained quite a reputation at Kahshahpiwi. Whenever his weekly supply of groceries was flown in, O'Reilly would climb out of the tower and stand on his head, clad only in a jock strap! This ritual continued until the pilot brought one of the park's female office workers along for the flight, and Gerry was mortified to hear her voice on the radio after his 'show.'

Kahshahpiwi Tower cabin.

While the ranger patrols were waning, rangers continued to staff the park's network of entry stations. Unlike earlier years, when the Valleys had such a battle to obtain their ranger posting, husband-and-wife teams were now becoming more common. For example, in 1967, Don and Thora McClure were assigned to the Cache Bay station, at the park's southeastern corner. Thora recalled: "The first people would come to Cache Bay when there was still ice around. They used to come from all over...They'd be so cold there would be ice on their mitts. But, oh, you know, fishermen are crazy!"

There was also Interior work to meet the park's recreational needs: in 1955, Quetico's first portage crew was hired. Bob Green and Jim Johnston, both Fort Frances men, were sent out that summer charged with maintaining the park's busy portages.

Don McClure, Cache Bay Ranger. Don was remembered for his many jokes...at dawn, he would play "Reveille" on his trumpet, waking up any campers in Cache Bay. **[Don McClure Collection]**

*Don McClure's wife Thora feeding a chipmunk at the Cache Bay Ranger Station. **[Don McClure Collection]***

Gerry O'Reilly asked to be allowed to work solo as a portage crewman, but Ross Williams refused. Instead, Williams wangled O'Reilly's appointment as Quetico's first park naturalist. Williams said, "We sent him down [east] to a couple of meetings, and as soon as he started to talk they knew he had ability. They hired him at Algonquin right away."

Of course, as more and more users flooded into the interior, more and more historic discoveries were made. For example, one party of campers discovered some crosses at the foot of the Badwater Portage -- the markers said, "Hereis [sic] C. Prim, R.W. Larcher, Died in Lumber Camp, No Known Relatives." Apparently, the two men had died at one of Shevlin-Clarke's camps in the late 1920s.

The portage from West Bay of Quetico Lake to Badwater Lake is always a challenge.

Barge used during the period of the Dawson Route (1870-79). This barge is currently underwater in Doré Lake near the Deux-Rivières Portage to Twin Lakes. Photo taken in 1970s.

Roger Thew in 1988.

Canadian visitors could now 'buy Canadian,' as Roger Thew had just become the first Canadian outfitter on the north side of Quetico. Steep Rock President M.S. Fotheringham had encouraged Thew -- a former Steep Rock employee -- to go into the business. Thew built his business along the Atikokan Highway, where other lodges and businesses would soon take root. The province expected even bigger development once the Atikokan Highway was extended to Fort Frances. The Quetico Foundation's *Newsletter* commented: "When completed, the 92-mile road will afford easy access to Quetico Park for visitors from the Prairies and the American Middle West. In anticipation, the Department of Lands and Forests has done some work this spring on improving an access road from Flanders (now reached only by the CNR) to Beaverhouse Lake where facilities comparable to those at French Lake are planned." (The Beaverhouse developments have not come to pass.)

Joe Kaliska worked on the Beaverhouse access road. He remembered:

> *We had to haul all the equipment in, trucks and graders and everything by rail. There was one camp at*

Aerial view of the new Thunder Bay-Atikokan highway, 1958.
[Kidd Collection]

Surprise Creek to do the brushing and one crew at Flanders on the construction. It was a winter works project.

In most places, we were following the old Shevlin-Clarke logging road to Lac La Croix. It was April and the frost was coming out of the ground and one day the whole right of way 150 feet wide started breaking up and started turning over. Muskeg came up from 20 feet down. The smell that came out of there from that muskeg! When it turned over [a] 20-inch diameter culvert disappeared and we were never able to locate it.

*Ross Williams adjusts the fire hazard sign at the Lac La Croix ranger station. This cabin was in use from the 1930s until 1967. It was taken down in 1971. In 1996, former ranger Joe Meany recalled: "When Vera and I took over this station in 1971, the old ranger station was still standing. Ross Williams said to take it down. [I] wanted to keep it for the portage crews and people caught in bad weather. Ross said, 'This is a government station and not a stop-over for wandering tourists, take it down.' Ross came in the following Wednesday. I watched him come up the walk and stop and look at where the building once stood. He looked at me, and walked by quickly, saying, 'That's better.' But on his way out, he walked part way over to the old site, he stood there for a while, then put his head down and walked back to the plane. I can only guess at what he was remembering." [**Nick Nickels Collection**]*

As recreational use of the park grew, so did interest in Quetico's natural and human history. The Quetico Foundation undertook a five-year program of publicity and educational work, to culminate with the park's 50th anniversary in 1959. The Foundation sponsored scientific research by Dr. V.B. Meen, on the geology of the park; R.C. Dailey, on the aboriginal heritage of Quetico; and Ken Kidd (the curator of ethnology at the Royal Ontario Museum) and Selwyn Dewdney, who investigated the park's aboriginal pictographs. Kidd and Dewdney later published their findings in *Indian Rock Paintings of the Great Lakes*.

Lac La Croix Ranger Station beach and boathouse in 1955. **[Kidd Collection].**

Loading Dr. Vic Meen's canoe on a Beaver aircraft at Lac La Croix in 1955. **[Frank Dumeney Collection]**

Left to right: Ken Kidd, ranger Frank Dumeney, Martha Kidd, and Doug Turner. 1955. **[Frank Dumeney Collection]**

Park Ranger Frank Dumeney lying on porch of the ranger cabin at Lookout Island, Pickerel Lake, 03 September 1955. **[Kidd Collection]**

Kidd and his wife, photographer Martha Kidd, toured the old Dawson Trail route and other areas of the park. The Kidds found scattered signs of the Trail (including an old boiler plate from a steamboat), remains of the old McLaurin trading post on Sturgeon Lake, and many historic artifacts of the Ojibwe people -- most importantly, the pictographs on the Painted Rock at Lac La Croix. Martha's photos of this trip and several subsequent trips were donated to the park collection. Ken Kidd called Quetico "one of the most striking examples of the forest primeval left in the world today."

Don Lageree, a ranger at Sturgeon cabin in 1955. It was in use from 1931 until 1980, and was home to a towerman. The steel tower across the lake was constructed in 1928. During the winter months, Sturgeon cabin was used as a park ranger patrol cabin. The last towerman was Roy Brown in 1957. When air patrols replaced the towers, the cabin became a base for the Quetico portage crews on their summer circuits. **[Kidd Collection]**

The Foundation published several new works from this research, including Meen's *Quetico Geology, Indians of Quetico* by Coatsworth and *Canoe Trails Through Quetico* by Keith Denis. The Foundation also hired filmmaker Christopher Chapman to make a new

185

film, *Quetico*, about the park. In turn, Chapman hired the youthful Bill Mason to play the central character. James Raffan commented in *Fire in the Bones*: "Being with Christopher Chapman in the field...had an air of excitement for Bill only eclipsed by his first viewing of the product...Bill was overcome with emotion."

Log remains at McLaurin's Post island on Sturgeon Lake in August 1963. [Kidd Collection]

The naturalist Claude Garton also undertook an inventory of the plants in the northern section of the park. A naturalist program began at French Lake, where Warren Sirrs and Jim Farr worked at the first, temporary park museum.

Frank Dumeney with the boiler plate from a steamer used in the Dawson Route era found at the top of the Maligne River; in 1955, it was being used at Sturgeon Sandspit as a fire grill.
[Frank Dumeney Collection]

Lac La Croix village from the water in 1956. The first Lac La Croix school is in the background on the left. John Boshey's old house is below the teacher's house and left of his new house (the white building). **[Harry Readman Collection]**

*The late Agnes Sox and her granddaughter Bernice Geyshick mending a fishing net at Lac La Croix, 1950s. **[Bruce Litteljohn Collection]***

Discussion of an international agreement on the Quetico-Superior returned to the table in 1955, when an international conference was held at the Quetico-Superior Wilderness Research Centre at Basswood Lake. Canadian and American officials met, and progress was made. In *Protected Places*, Gerald Killan writes, "Even the Foundation's American ally, the President's Quetico-Superior Committee, convinced provincial officials of its good intentions. Beginning with a meeting at Basswood Lake in 1955, Charles S. Kelly, chairman of the President's committee, greatly influenced Ben Greenwood and other [Lands and Forests] personnel by mapping out the progress made by the American government in reclaiming the alienated lands within the roadless areas of the Superior National Forest."

Quetico-Superior Wilderness Research Centre on the U.S. side of Basswood Lake.

Frank Hubachek on the left, with his law partner Charles S. Kelly.

Donald O' Hearn portaging around Lower Basswood Falls in 1954.
He resigned as Executive Secretary of the Quetico Foundation in 1955.
[Don O'Hearn Collection]

At the time of the Conference, a fire started on the Canadian side. Ross Williams -- who was attending the conference -- suspected that the fire had been set to test Canadian-American co-operation on fire suppression. In fact, it wasn't, but that didn't stop a strange chain of events. Williams recalled:

> *"That was the time of the Fire. We were going past [Cabin] 16 and I stopped to see if there were any messages. 'All Beaver aircraft are grounded. There's a crack in the struts and all the Beavers in the world are grounded, Australia, Canada, etc.' So we went down to Prairie Portage, I think, and [when] we were coming*

back...I saw this smoke. I said, 'Oh no, I better go back [to Prairie Portage]...' I radioed Nym Lake and said, 'There's a fire.' They said, 'We can't come, all the planes are grounded.' So the head of the USFS [United States Forest Service] was there [at the conference], and he got the USFS to fly in and fight the fire. [They hadn't yet been informed of the order.] I said I had to get over there. So I went over there and found the Americans fighting the fire. About two hours later, the Canadians arrived in a chartered aircraft, but the Americans had it out by this time. It looked like it was a set-up job, but it was a lightning strike back in the bush. [Charles] Kelly got a kick out of that."

The then-Minister of Lands and Forests, Kelso Roberts, ordered a plane to pick him up, and he was also frustrated by the grounding order.

After the 1955 Conference, leading members of the Quetico Foundation hoped an international agreement could be reached. Eventually, that agreement took the form of an exchange of diplomatic letters between Washington and Toronto. Premier Leslie Frost said the two governments agreed to "a friendly co-operation, without binding any side to any policy." They would consult with each other at the field level and keep each other informed of changes. Quetico's growing number of allies accepted this small victory -- a long way from the International Peace Forest proposal of earlier years, but a commitment on paper regardless.

The province's commitment would be tested.

The Battle for Wilderness

In the late '60s and early '70s, Quetico would become the flash-point for a province-wide debate: what is the purpose of a park? What should it be? Is it a reserve of resources, to be used if needed? Or, is a park a *preserve*, to be untouched in any way? Is resource use compatible with wilderness?

This was not a minor debating point -- Quetico's purpose, and the purpose of many other provincial parks, was in question.

The tide of new recreational users had forced the issue. As far back as 1962, the Interpretive Supervisor of Ontario Provincial Parks, A.F. Helmsley, warned that: "The demand for outdoor recreational space has been prominent in the organization and development of Ontario's provincial park system...[but] there is a danger point when crowding destroys the purpose and the environment suffers from overuse. Wilderness recreation has a low carrying capacity because the requirements are solitude and quiet -- an environment for inspirational enjoyment and the sense of personal achievement. If this form of recreation is to survive the interiors of such parks as Quetico, Algonquin, Lake Superior and Sibley (Sleeping Giant) must be reserved as they are. Controls become necessary: on access roads, on lumbering, on indiscriminate aircraft entry, on outboard motors and powerboats."

The province had moved to curb some of the problems. In 1965, Deputy Minister Frank MacDougall approved several measures to further protect Quetico, including: the continued reservation of Hunter Island from commercial logging; the creation of 'skyline reserves' along water routes, replacing the old 400 foot shoreline allowances; prohibition of watercraft with overnight accommodation (such as houseboats); and the purchase of all outstanding mining patents in the park.

Two years later, the province unveiled a new "classification system" for provincial parks. This was one of the biggest changes in the history of the park system, as a comprehensive set of rules would exist for all parks in each of five classes -- Primitive, Wild River, Natural

Environment, Recreation, and Nature Reserve. (A "Historic" class was later created.) Within each park, different 'zones' would be set aside for different uses, with the acceptable uses determined by the park's class. Quetico was placed in the "Natural Environment" category.

These actions won public support, but overuse problems continued to snowball. Visitors to Quetico began to complain of overcrowding, littering and basic disrespect of the park. In the fall of 1963, the entire park ranging crew had to be put on garbage detail on Pickerel Lake and several adjoining lakes. The following year, Rainy River District Forester Ron Balkwill wrote to a park visitor that his department's greatest problem was "trying to keep the portages and campsites clean. ...The greatest hazard of all, the disposable glass beer bottle, has only been with us for a couple of years but the broken glass will be there for generations." Quetico was becoming a victim of its own recreational success.

The resumption of commercial logging in Quetico also galvanized park supporters into action. After a twenty-year pause, the Jim Mathieu Lumber Company was ready to resume cutting in the park -- the grandson of J.A. Mathieu obtained a license to log the northeast side of Quetico Park. Camp 111 was to be built at Baptism Creek, with logs sent out to the company's mill at Sapawe. Pulpwood would be shipped out to Thunder Bay via Kawene.

Mathieu began the cutting, but the company went into receivership in 1967 and was taken over by forestry giant Domtar. Domtar and an American company, the Ontario-Minnesota Pulp and Paper Company, now had logging rights to large areas in the northwestern and northeastern parts of the park.

Obviously, logging was not new to Quetico -- the concept of 'multiple uses' for parks had been widely accepted as long as there had been provincial parks in Ontario. In many cases, groups supporting Quetico had criticized the particulars of logging in the park, not the presence of the timber companies themselves. Three generations of men in the Rainy River District had earned a living from Quetico's timber.

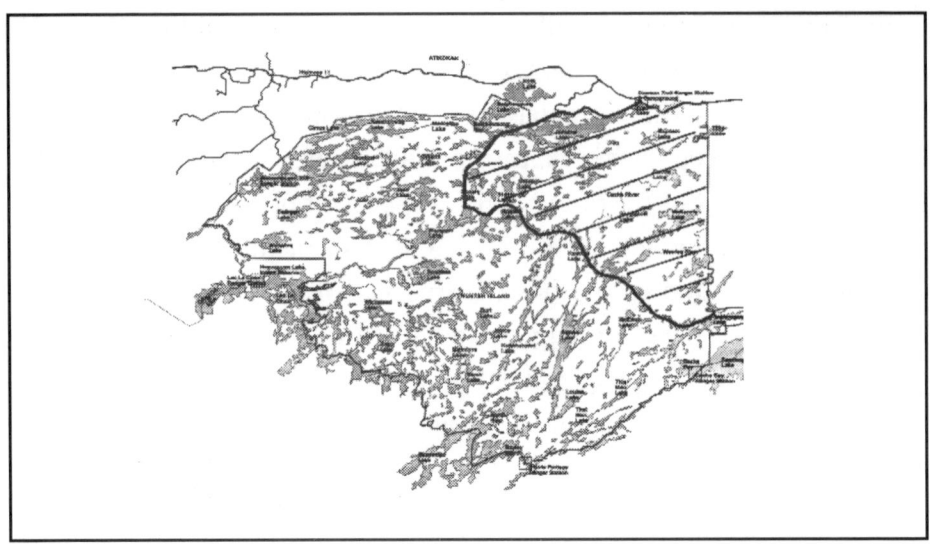

The Jim Mathieu limit D-2291 in Quetico Park.

*Bruce Litteljohn. [**Bruce Litteljohn Collection**]*

194

However, there was now a sea change in public attitudes: for some, logging and wilderness became incompatible. In 1984, Bruce Litteljohn said: "I wasn't opposed in general to logging in the park at that point. What I was opposed to was, that...particular company was breaking all kinds of specific rules. They were dropping trees right into Baptism Creek which was advertised as a canoe route. I remember trying to walk up the portages toward Baptism Lake and they were just a mess, there was slash all over and high stumps."

Members of the Quetico Advisory Committee. Standing left to right: H. Alan Tibbetts, James H. Jessiman, Andrew Jourdain, John E. Stokes, Dr. Antonius Lovink, Alexander Phillips, Harold S. Braun, John B. Ridley, T. Patrick Reid. Seated left to right: Robert T. Thomson, Clifford McIntosh, Sydney G. Hancock, Dr. Albert E. Berry.

The issue of logging in Quetico caught fire when logging reached deeper into the park. The intense public reaction against this move put a tremendous amount of heat on the Conservative administration of John Robarts. With the participation of the Algonquin Wildlands League, a major public campaign began to have Quetico reclassified from a "Natural Environment" park to a "Primitive" park. In Primitive parks, logging was totally banned.

René Brunelle, the Lands and Forests minister, gamely defended his government's policy, but concessions were won on several fronts. Quetico's logging regulations were tightened. Brunelle also created an Advisory Committee on Quetico, which would spend the next two years soliciting public comments on the future of the park. For the first time, the membership represented the public, not just interest groups. The government had already formed a committee to advise on Algonquin Provincial Park.

Fergy Wilson was the secretary of a government task force assigned to give information to the Quetico committee. (Wilson later served as Quetico Superintendent under Dave Elder.) He commented: "The Ministry gave the Quetico Advisory Committee two years to get their job done, including a public participation program. It was their job to take all the information and to think about it, tear it apart and put it back together again, and come up with some specific recommendations for the future of Quetico Park -- what kind of park it should be, what class of park, the management policies and guidelines that should govern the management of Quetico in the future."

The Committee received a flood of comments, including 4 500 letters and more than 400 briefs. Only 30 of the 4 500 letters were sent in support of continued logging. Spontaneously, large public meetings across the province drew strong public support for wilderness preservation in Quetico, even from people who had never seen the park. For them, the continued existence of wilderness was the paramount issue.

Syd Hancock, the chairman of the Committee and Reeve of Atikokan, later commented: "It's that big mass of people in the southern part of the province that really shapes political perspectives...the mood of the times...was one of not exploiting resources, being more gentle on the earth. All those ideas started to come out then. And they were the avant-garde ideas, and [Conservative Premier Bill] Davis's government at that time was an avant-garde government. ...See that was all part of that time and this park idea was part of the same time in which people were looking for better ways of doing things. It was also a time when people had a romantic notion of the outdoors."

Gerald Killan writes that "Once rekindled, the Quetico controversy grew into the most intense struggle of the wilderness preservation campaign and became a symbol of the new environmental awareness in Ontario society."

The anti-logging die was now cast, but it was a difficult decision. Fergy Wilson said: "The future of the Sapawe mill was a large concern to the Committee. The Committee wanted to be sure that the mill would not be adversely affected and Atikokan would not be affected by making a decision to eliminate logging.

"The Committee, as I remember, was unanimously agreeing to make that recommendation to the Minister to stop logging. Some of them agreed to it because they felt philosophically that it was the best thing to do, and a number of them agreed to it because they'd been assured that there were alternate sources of wood available and the operation of the mill would not suffer so they saw that as an opportunity to make that kind of a decision, that it wasn't black or white in the sense that we could have wilderness and no jobs or we could cut trees and have jobs. What they found is that they could have their cake and eat it too."

This possibility only became clear when the Deputy Minister of Lands and Forests stated publicly that commercially viable wood supplies were available outside Quetico. A scientific study by Arthur Boissonneau also cast doubt on the quality of Quetico's timber resources.

In May 1971, the Committee wrote that it could "report without hesitation that the vast majority of [the presentations] stressed the wilderness aspect of the Park's future and in particular the elimination of commercial logging.

"In view of our interpretation of the public's desires, and on the basis of information we now have available, the Committee unanimously recommends to you:

197

(a) That as soon as possible commercial logging within the boundaries of Quetico Park be eliminated, subject to the provision that the Government provide alternate areas outside the limits of Quetico Park for the Jim Mathieu Lumber Limited (Domtar)..."

The new government of Bill Davis agreed. On 13 May 1971, Davis announced that logging would be banned from Quetico. Ontario-Minnesota's cutting rights were terminated and Domtar had to relocate its operations outside Quetico.

However, it would be two more years before the province agreed to move Quetico into the "Primitive" class of parks. The change came after the Quetico Advisory Committee submitted a proposed "Master Plan" for Quetico to the government. Such plans were to be instituted for all Ontario parks, bringing order to decades of ad-hoc administrative decisions. The government's decision on the plan was announced in June 1973. In *Protected Places*, Gerald Killan writes that Leo Bernier, the Minister of Natural Resources, announced that:

> *Logging, mining and hunting would be prohibited. Boundaries would be adjusted to conform [to] natural water limits, and buffer zones would be created around the park. Additional access points from the north would be developed, both as a means of stimulating tourism in the northwestern region and of relieving user pressure on congested canoe routes near the international border. Daily visitor quota systems at each access point would also reduce interior user pressures on the crowded waterways and encourage the use of the northern entry points. A can and bottle ban, a policy introduced in the Boundary Waters Canoe Area of the Superior National Forest in May 1971, would also be instituted in Quetico to control the mounting litter problem. Eventually, Bernier promised, outboard motors would also be*

prohibited, but the policy would be phased in, to reduce the impact it would have on the livelihoods of the Lac La Croix Indian band, who served as guides in the park. Although the motorboat ban would not apply on certain lakes for an interim period, motors would be immediately restricted to ten horsepower. Trapping rights would also be granted only to aboriginal peoples; however, all other owners of registered traplines would be allowed to work their lines until they chose to abandon them. "These new policies," Bernier predicted, "will do much to reduce user conflicts and will establish long-term protection for this important natural resource in Northern Ontario."

In 1972, the Quetico Park Advisory Committee visits the Lac La Croix Indian reserve. A gathering in the High School auditorium included John Boshey, John Ottertail and Leon Jourdain.

John Boshey, Chief of the Lac La Croix First Nation from 1957-74, wearing the silver Treaty Medal given to commemorate the signing of Treaty Three in 1873.

Dave Elder: 1973-1987

The battle to save Quetico's wilderness had been won. However, an equally difficult campaign lay ahead: the battle to *manage* the wilderness. It was a battle of details and compromises, each of which would affect the park in the next three decades.

To wage this campaign, a new captain was put at Quetico's helm. Under re-organization, the old Department of Lands and Forests became the Ministry of Natural Resources. Ross Williams was promoted to a new position at Nipigon, and Dave Elder became Lands and Parks Supervisor and the Superintendent of Quetico.

Dave Elder, Quetico Park Superintendent (1973-1975, 1984-1987), Land and Parks Supervisor (1973-1987).

Dave was always keen to learn all he could about Quetico. He fully supported any project that would add to knowledge of the park.

201

His fields of interest were as broad as the park's horizons: archaeology, botany, fur trade history, geology, and zoology were all areas that felt his support. And, of course, his great love of birds is well known by anyone ever associated with him. Many of the park's bird records are attributable to his excellent observation and identification skills. He canoed through the park whenever his busy schedule would allow, and spent time at all the entry stations, asking questions of both canoeists and station attendants.

Mike Barker, Atikokan District Manager (1973-1979).

One of the first tasks on Elder's desk was the proposed Quetico Master Plan. Mike Barker, then the new Atikokan District Manager for the Ministry of Natural Resources, recalled: "In 1973, we were handed a set of things that said we want a motor ban, we want a bottle and can ban and we want a quota system...develop new entry points...change the use pattern by having fewer people come into the south and more in the north. The Master Plan had to be prepared and so luckily we had Dave Elder, a star performer and guy who is renowned for his abilities to get on with things and for his ability to understand the way parks should be managed. And so he and Dale Smith, a park planner from Thunder Bay office, sat down in the fall of 1973 and began to write up the Park Master Plan. By July 1974, they had the first draft virtually written. It took from July 1974 to September 1977 to polish it, adjust it and most of that time was spent in getting approval at the various levels. Dave should take total and full credit for the master plan because that's a major contribution."

That Master Plan eventually won a Conservation Award from the Federation of Ontario Naturalists, and Dave was selected to receive it on behalf of the government.

At the core of the plan was a determination to co-exist with the Lac La Croix First Nation People. Some attempts had been made to broker a deal between both interests. For example, trap lines had been permitted in the northwestern sections of the park so that the Lac La Croix people could continue to earn income. The new Master Plan allowed trapping to continue.

A Lac La Croix guide and passenger in a motorized canoe, Beaverhouse Lake.

In 1979, a total ban on all motors was put into effect, with the exception that in Quetico Provincial Park, a member of the Lac La Croix Indian Band who was also a member of the Lac La Croix Guides Association could operate a power boat with an engine rating not exceeding 10 horsepower. These motors could be used on Quetico, Beaverhouse, Wolseley, Tanner, Minn, and McAree lakes, or the Maligne River from Lac La Croix to Tanner Lake.

The exception meant professional guides at the Lac La Croix First Nation could continue their work -- the argument was made, successfully, that many band members' livelihoods depended on this decision.

In addition, Quetico's southwestern boundary was changed to move all the Canadian waters of Lac La Croix *out* of the park. This meant motorboat access could continue on the Canadian side of Lac La Croix without contravention of the ban. (No motors were allowed on the U.S. side of Lac La Croix which was part of the Boundary Waters Canoe Area.) The U.S. State Department supported this action, though some questioned whether it was a violation of the Webster-Ashburton Treaty on the U.S.-Canada boundary waters. (The federal government stated the regulations did not violate Webster-Ashburton.)

One of the most important voices in support of the motor ban was Charlie Ericksen (see color insert), operator of the Nym Lake Voyageur Wilderness Programme. A long-time opponent of logging in Quetico, Charlie's company organized canoe trips into Quetico for American students. His uncompromising advocacy of wilderness values grated on some, but he continued to make his case until the very end. Only two days before his death in October 1977, Ericksen attended a meeting of the Provincial Parks Council in Atikokan to demand outboard motors be eliminated from the park altogether.

At that time, many changes were made on the park's eastern, northern and western perimeter, so that the boundary came no closer than 600 feet to any park lake. This meant no lake could overlap the boundaries, so Saganagons Lake was brought entirely within park jurisdiction, as were Mack, Batchewaung and Cirrus lakes. Several others, including Tilly and Bitchu, were excluded from Quetico. This made enforcement of the park rules much simpler, as anyone on a given lake or river now had to follow the same regulations. Between 1975 and 1977, the new boundary was surveyed and then cleared of trees for a width of 20 feet.

A tremendous amount of research, study and simple exploration of Quetico during the 1970s led to many new discoveries. One of the most important was the role of fire in the natural life cycle of the forest. From 1975 to 1977, a fire ecology study was completed by G.T. Woods and R.J. Day. The Quetico Master Plan (then still in the works) declared that certain natural processes, including fire, would *not* be allowed to run unchecked in Quetico. However, the studies found that about 90 per cent of the plant communities in the park were 'pioneer' species, found in areas touched by fire.

Before 1920, each area of the park could expect to be affected by fire within a 78-year cycle -- since 1940, that had increased to an 807-year cycle. This was probably the result of modern fire suppression, which, eventually, would result in a major change to the composition of the forest, as the 'pioneer' forest would be replaced by hardwood and balsam fir. The studies recommended burning 12 000 to 15 000 acres of the park each year. Forester Mike Barker commented: "If we don't start burning soon the character of the forest will change and then it won't be the same park that makes it so attractive to people now. If we don't burn we'll lose the pines. It may take 80 years but we'll lose them. ...There'll be such vast amounts of dead and dying and dry fuel down there that when fires do start, they'll be uncontrollable." The debate over controlled burning would continue.

Other work produced important results. In 1974 alone, more than 137 new aboriginal historic sites were located. Many aboriginal artifacts were found, including a cache of birch bark scrolls, knife and spear points, and ancient siltstone quarries along Knife Lake. Bryan Molineaux surveyed 15 of the park's pictograph sites, and found most of them in good condition.

The plants and animals came under scrutiny from scientists. The Royal Ontario Museum sent a team (supervised by David Nagorsen) to study the park's small mammals. They discovered such rare rodents as the Rock Vole and the Heather Vole.

Left to right: Paul Money, Jon Nelson and David Nagorsen at the Beaverhouse dock

Tornado damage on the portage from Mack Lake to Home Lake, photographed during the naturalist orientation canoe trip of June 1979. The Rock Vole was found on this portage.

Bob Burns, Conservation officer, on the beach at the Lac La Croix Ranger Station. Bob came to the Atikokan District in 1972. In 1977, Bob was appointed Zone Manager in the Basswood lake area of Quetico. His enthusiasm was infectious and his crew began to prepare an inventory of every campsite and portage in the zone. Bob then went to work full-time in the Fish and Wildlife Branch.

Shan Walshe at the top of portage out of Mack Lake to Home Lake. It wasn't possible to hurry on a trip with Shan in Quetico.

On one of his many canoe expeditions into the park, Shan Walshe discovered a plant previously not documented in Ontario, the inland rush (*juncus interior*) -- it is a species of the dry Great Plains of North America, found from Texas north to Alberta. Walshe's many years of work in Quetico eventually produced the book *Plants of Quetico and the Ontario Shield*, still one of the most important scientific works on the park.

On another trip, out along Crooked Lake Walshe had a chance encounter with one of the legendary figures of Quetico: Bill Magie.

Wilderness Voices: Bill Magie

Bill Magie (see color insert) was truly a voice of, and for, wilderness. A life-long champion of conservation, Magie began travelling in Quetico from its earliest days. As far back as 1910, Magie (not to be confused with Billy *Magee*) became a regular summer visitor to the lakes. He started guiding in 1922 and continued to guide well into his seventies. Magie once said, "I'll guide as long as I can work -- cook a meal and all those things...The old days are gone forever, never to return, but I was lucky. I was there during the good years."

There is no better testimonial of Bill's influence than this one, written in July 1979 by Shan Walshe:

In May, Shirley Peruniak and I drove to Eau Claire Lakes, Wisconsin to interview the famous Quetico Park guide and conservationist, 76-year-old Bill Magie. Though gravely ill, Bill jumped off the bed to greet us, dressed in bush clothes and leather boots, his sparkling eyes shouting defiance at his illness.

Bill's father, Dr. William H. Magie of Duluth, chief surgeon for all the railroad, lumber, and mining companies in Northeastern Minnesota, gained fame by performing the first appendectomy in Duluth. He was also a close friend of Theodore Roosevelt and Herbert Hoover.

208

Bill Magie and his brother John in pajamas at Curtain Falls, 1909.
[Bill Magie Collection]

In 1909, at the age of seven years, Bill had his first opportunity to visit the Quetico country. A large red pine log had fallen off a car on the four-mile railway connecting Fall and Basswood lakes, severely injuring a top lumber company executive. A special train was dispatched from Duluth, bringing Dr. Magie, accompanied by seven-year-old Bill. During the 18 1/2 hr. trip, young Bill had a great time helping the engineer run the engine. Though the rescue mission was a failure, the injured man having died on Fall Lake en route to Winton, Dr. Magie and Bill were invited to go on a canoe trip in the Boundary Waters Canoe Area. Because most of the lakes in the B.W.C.A. were jammed with logs due to the tremendous logging activity taking place at that time, they decided to visit Quetico instead, paddling through North Bay of Basswood, Burke, Sunday, Poacher, back to Basswood and then over the four-mile portage to Fall Lake and Winton.

From 1912 to 1922 Bill went on a canoe trip to Quetico each year, first with his father and later with high school and college students supervised by a teacher named Philips. When Philips had a heart attack in 1922, Bill, himself, assumed leadership of the annual trips.

"Black sheep Bill" did not take kindly to routine and discipline. Subjected to stints at several preparatory schools and colleges, including the Virginia Military Institute, he was expelled from each in turn for some misdemeanor or other. Bill and Joe Mayo (of Mayo Clinic fame) were suspended from Princeton for inviting two Follies stars to a university dance. At another college he was a classmate of Reggie Vanderbilt, who persuaded him to buy a Stuts Bearcat automobile and send the bill to his father!

Obtaining his pilot's license from Orville Wright, he flew a souped-up Jenny (Curtis N-4, a stick-and-wire biplane) in from over Lake Superior, under the Duluth aerial lift bridge, did an Immelman (a half-loop with a 180-degree twist on top) and flew back over the bridge -- all this on a $50 bet! The Duluth municipal authorities were quite perplexed when they discovered there were no city bylaws prohibiting such a stunt.

Finally graduating from the University of Virginia as a mining engineer in 1925, Bill got a job with U.S. Steel at Coleraine, driving back and forth to Duluth on weekends in his Stutz Bearcat. His heart was in the Quetico, however, and in 1926 he jumped at the offer of a job with the International Joint Commission, supervising a survey crew charged with the task of accurately marking the Minnesota-Ontario border. Bigwigs from Washington frequently visited the survey camps in summer under the pretext of inspecting the border (they really had come to fish!)

One day while eating illegal moose meat, a visiting official asked what type of meat tasted so good. Quick-witted Bill promptly replied "pine beef."

During his days with the survey crew, Bill got to know Bill Darby, Jeff Seeley, Gunder Graves and other rangers stationed along the southern border of Quetico Park (a picture of Bill and his survey crew hangs in Cabin 16 on Basswood Lake). [It remained there until the closure of Cabin 16 in 1980.] During the summer of 1926 Bill saw only two other parties along the entire length of the southern border of Quetico. In March, 1929 went [sic] from Kenora to Warroad, Minnesota by dog team to complete the survey by tying it into the Norman Dam.

Left to right: Park rangers Tom Quinn and Ted Dettbarn, with R. Willis, Bill Magie and Carl Lindy. R. Willis, Bill Magie and Carl Lindy were on the U.S. Corps of Engineers water level survey team for Basswood Lake in 1926. They stayed with Quetico park rangers at Cabin 16. ***[Bill Magie Collection]***

From 1929 to 1933 Bill flew a mail run for the Stinson and Curtis Wright Aircraft Company. When the mail contract was cancelled during the depths of the depression in 1933, Bill acted as a guide on an 11-week canoe trip through the Quetico with a side trip to Port Arthur (Thunder Bay) to buy five cases of whiskey for his client (Canada went wet in 1927). Three of these arrived intact at Ely, after having been carried over every portage across Quetico Park.

During the depression years 1933-41 Bill worked for the U.S. Forest Service in Superior National Forest in various Civilian

211

Conservation Corps camps, fixing docks, building roads, portages, etc. After a stint in the U.S. marines during the Second World War, he worked in the Hibbing Iron Mines as an engineering inspector from 1945 to 1962.

Receiving his pension in 1962, Bill again heeded the call of the canoe country and Quetico, working out of Ely as a guide for Bill Rom Outfitters from 1964-78. During these years he guided such famous people as Zsa Zsa Gabor...and, in 1978, Dr. Anne La Bastille, author of "Woodswoman."

Bill avoids bear trouble by taking along his 15-year-old springer spaniel, Murphy, who has, to date, accompanied him on 130 canoe trips.

At Christmas, 1977, 74-year-old Bill, accompanied only by Murphy, flew to Powell Lake, just east of the Quetico Boundary and walked by snowshoe to the Gunflint Trail via Mack, Munro, Cullen, Ross, Bitchu, Saganagons, and Saganaga lakes, accomplishing a feat many men half his age would never dare.

...One of the founders of the Wilderness Society in 1949, Bill acted as executive secretary for many years. Much of his life has been spent trying to protect the canoe country of the B.W.C.A. and Quetico from commercial exploitation and the inroads of civilization. He once even travelled to Washington to meet with President Kennedy to push the B.W.C.A. Wilderness Bill of 1964.

All present and former Quetico Park rangers and staff join with me in wishing Bill fortitude in his illness and saluting him for his years of service as "watch-dog of the wilderness."

In 1979, the watch-dog of the wilderness was honored with a bronze plaque at the edge of the country he loved so much. The plaque reads: "Think on this land of lakes and forests/It cannot survive Man's greed/Without Man's selfless dedication."

Fergy Wilson: 1975-1983

While the first Quetico Master Plan took shape, Fergy Wilson took over as Superintendent of the park in 1975. A graduate of the School of Forestry at the University of Toronto, Wilson came to the job with a great deal of experience in the bush: he had worked as Quetico's Park Naturalist, and had been Parks Supervisor for the Fort Frances District.

Fergy Wilson, Superintendent of Quetico Park, 1975-1983.

One of the most important moves made during Fergy's tenure was the park quota system. Created with help from staff of the Boundary Waters Canoe Area -- where a quota system went into effect in 1974 -- the new rules limited the total number of people who could visit Quetico's interior each year. By 1980, this plan caused a significant reduction in traffic at some entry stations: for example, entries at the Prairie Portage station dropped by about one-third. The quotas were necessary "to protect certain areas of the park against overuse," the government announced. Certain areas really were experiencing the effects of overuse: for example, portages in the Basswood Lake zone were becoming so eroded that erosion 'bars' had to be installed. Laid perpendicular to the trail, the bars prevented the soil and rocks from being carried away.

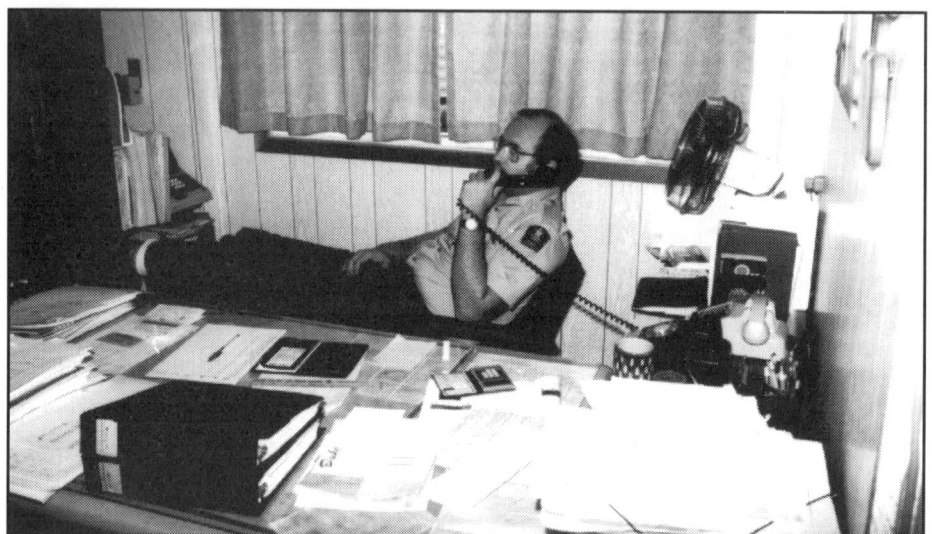

Superintendent Fergy Wilson in his office at Park headquarters at Nym Lake.

The quota system helped direct a little more traffic to the park's northern side, where -- according to a study by Mario Madau of the University of Waterloo -- Quetico-related tourism was putting almost two and a half million dollars into Atikokan's economy each year. Among the many tourists on the north side was the conqueror of Mount Everest, Sir Edmund Hillary. Hillary visited Beaverhouse Lake in 1979 to test some new camping equipment.

Erosion bars in place on a portage.

Wilbur Hyatt, station ranger at Cabin 16, assistant park naturalist Shirley Peruniak and Superintendent Fergy Wilson.

1983 August meeting with Quetico-Superior staff sharing problems and ideas. During Dave Elder's period, there was increasing consultation and co-operation between Quetico Park staff and personnel from the U.S. Forest Service and the Minnesota Department of Natural Resources.

Dave Elder, George Halemba and parks clerk Mary McKay in the park office at Nym Lake in the late 1970s.

Other restrictions further protected the Quetico environment. For example, snowmobiles were banned outright, as were "non-burnable, disposable food and beverage containers and eating utensils within the interior of Quetico Provincial Park." This helped solve the park's garbage problem. Mike Barker recalled: "The park is clean now. It was pretty clean in 1973 as a matter of fact. Ross Williams should take the credit for cleaning the park. If anyone deserves credit...it's the people under Ross Williams' administration because they spent five or six years doing nothing but haul 50 years of garbage out of that park, to the point where by 1973 it was really, well, I didn't find it all that offensive in my first trip."

However, Wilson also had to oversee many cutbacks at Quetico, as the provincial government 'tightened its belt.' In 1976, the Kahshahpiwi Fire Tower was shut down, and in 1980, the entry stations at Cabin 16 and Prairie Portage were both closed. (This followed the closure of the Canada Customs posts at both locations.) Given that these were among the park's busiest entry stations, the closure generated many complaints. While the Prairie Portage station was ultimately re-opened, Cabin 16 was consigned to history.

Ranger station at Prairie Portage.

217

Prairie Portage Customs Station closed after the 1996 season, when the "Remote Area Border Crossing Permits" were used for entry into Quetico.

Wilbur and Bernice Hyatt standing by the Basswood Ranger Station sign at Cabin 16. They were station rangers there from 1967 until Cabin 16 closed in 1981. They subsequently worked at the Beaverhouse Ranger Station until 1985.

Cabin 16, Basswood Lake, built in 1938, closed in 1981 and still standing today.

Mary Kerr of the Ontario Provincial Parks Council boarding a Provincial aircraft in August 1981.

Sally Burns (l) and Laurie McCuaig (r), first female portage crew at Prairie Portage in 1978.

Prior to his departure from the park in 1983, Wilson's last major task was to implement recommendations from the first Quetico Master Plan Review. Once again, the public responded, sending more than 1,400 submissions to the government. The Ontario Provincial Parks Council reviewed the material and made its suggestions. In all, there were 14 recommendations, including:

- The maximum size of interior visiting parties was reduced from nine people to six. (This was later revoked.)
- Traplines in the park could not change ownership after May 1986- once the owner surrendered them, they were cancelled.

An exemption was made for trappers at Lac La Croix.

Still, the Park Goal remained the same: "...to preserve Quetico Provincial Park which contains an environment of geological, biolog- ical, cultural and recreational significance, in perpetuity for the people of Ontario as an area of wilderness that is not adversely affected by human activities."

With the departure of Fergy Wilson in 1983, Dave Elder was once again Quetico Park Superintendent and Lands and Parks Supervisor.

Sally Burns, portage crew. She later worked in the Quetico Interpretive Program.

Ontario Rangers (Junior Rangers) working on the shoreline at Prairie Portage.

Superintendent Dave Elder sitting behind his desk enjoying a joke with Assistant Superintendent Ed Hansson.

Portage crew and volunteers sitting in front of "Ranger Hall" at Lac La Croix Ranger Station in 1984. Joe and Vera Meany are in front.

Celebrating 75 Years

History was the over-riding theme in 1984, as Quetico Park celebrated its 75th anniversary.

To mark the event, Frank Jordan, Jr., John Ottertail, Shan Walshe and I paddled around the park. This is my own memoir of the trip:

> *"August 19th -- home at last! At 7 pm, as we beached the canoe, French Lake was a mirror reflecting a few canoes moving slowly in the evening sun. A gentle tail wind had helped us endure the 24-mile paddle from Russell Lake under a sweltering sun.*

John Ottertail and Frank Jordon, Jr., of Lac La Croix First Nation on a Heritage Canoe Trip on Saganagons Lake in 1984.

> *At Russell Rapids, where the water from Saganaga and Kawnipi empties into Sturgeon Lake, we said good-bye to John Ottertail and Frank Jordan, Jr. "It has been a good trip, and you are good people," John remarked.*

Shan and I watched as John's steady, quick paddle stroke pushed his canoe toward lower Sturgeon, the Maligne, and the Lac La Croix Reserve. Then we turned and headed north through Upper Sturgeon, back to the job of writing up Quetico's history.

Strange history's interconnecting links with the past! Years ago, in 1910, John's grandfather and namesake had guided an Ontario Game and Fisheries Commission over these same waters. When he was old and living on the Reserve, he had held John in his arms. Frank Jordan, Jr.'s grandfather, Jimmy, was a son of this same man. As we sat around the evening campfire, John had recalled memories of him.

Paddling north, I thought about the dark, moonless night when Shan [Walshe] had described the constellations of twinkling stars and John had told of his father, Charlie, showing him a constellation resembling the intestine of a rabbit.

*West side of Rebecca Falls. [**Bruce Litteljohn Collection**]*

The canoe trip had begun on August 10, 1984 at the Lac La Croix Ranger Station. (The night before, the drums of a pow-wow could be heard over the 15 miles of water separating the Ranger Station from the Reserve.) At 3 pm, the unlikely party of two office workers and two outboard motor guides, sons of the Ojibwe who had lived in this wilderness before it became a Forest Reserve, headed east into the park to celebrate Quetico's 75th anniversary.

Standing beside the foaming rapids at Rebecca Falls on Iron Lake, John remembered how, during a log drive in the 1940s, they had blocked the eastern channel and used the wider western one. And how, in 1931, when he was three, he was taken on a toboggan pulled by three dogs, when his family moved to a Shevlin-Clarke logging camp on Badwater Lake, at a time when the Depression had closed many of the camps.

*Curtain Falls. [**Oberholtzer Collection**]*

At Curtain Falls portage, he recalled guiding for the resorts located on Crooked Lake during the '40s and

'50s. And, while Shan showed some interesting plants to people on the portage, John told me how his father knew the medicine in each plant, but unfortunately [he] had not been interested. The memory sparked his enthusiasm, and he soon began telling stories to groups of canoeists encountered on the portages.

On the Canadian side of Crooked Lake he pointed out the wreckage of an old truck with wooden wheel spokes, which he said belonged to Shevlin-Clarke.

His excitement rose as we approached lower Basswood Falls (see color insert), a favourite fishing spot of the early Ojibwe. In the French Lake albums are photos of Indian families in 1915 as they travelled back and forth from Lac La Croix to Basswood Lake to visit relatives and go riceing at Jackfish Bay and work in logging camps on the U.S. side.

At the Horse Portage, John, remembering earlier trips, chose to follow the river, putting in and out several times, while Shan and I struggled over the entire one-mile distance in a single carry. Nevertheless, all of us were hot and tired when we finally reached the top of the falls at Basswood Lake.

As we ate lunch, we were amazed at John's unbelievable eyesight, when he spotted a deer grazing in a marsh on the far-away Canadian shore.

Pointing to the rocky, blueberry-covered ridges above U.S. Point, John suggested that Basswood Lake derived its name from the Ojibwe, bassi-min-an meaning "dried blueberry."

On Knife Lake we visited Dorothy Molter at her Isle of Pines retreat. How small we seemed under the white pines towering over her winter cabin. While we drank some of her home-made root beer, Dorothy brought out one of her old photograph albums of the early days when she first came to this country in 1930.

Dorothy Molter, last permanent resident of the Boundary Waters Canoe Area, died in December 1986, aged 79.

The wind was with us as we headed down Knife Lake the next morning to examine an ancient Indian quarry Shan had discovered in 1984. The ten-foot-high outcropping of siltstone, hidden in a stand of big cedars, possessed the qualities necessary for making stone tools, spear points, and knives. We experienced an eerie feeling, realizing that men laboured here thousands of years ago, shaping the stone until it was razor sharp.

Old maps gave the Indian name of the lake -- Mokoman -- meaning "knife," and the French translated it as "Lac des Couteaux."

Artifacts found in Quetico made from Knife Lake siltstone.

On a towering, orange-coloured cliff, looming over the waters of Ottertrack Lake, we made out the tracks of a giant otter embedded in solid rock. A rock outcropping, jutting out of a nearby hillside, had an uncanny resemblance to an Indian chief, forever guarding the Ottertrack cliff.

Here we discussed Shawbo-geezigoh, daughter of famous Chief Blackstone, chief at Lac La Croix after the treaty of 1873. Married to Nanekaconap, son of Kabaigon, first chief of the Kawa Bay Reserve, she regularly left small gifts in a crevice at the foot of the sacred cliff.

Lake Saganaga held special significance for John. As a boy, he journeyed to this lake with his family to visit relatives and collect wild rice in nearby waters, later returning home to Lac la Croix with hundreds of pounds of rice.

At Cache Bay Ranger Station, at the east end of Saganaga, we enjoyed a delicious roast beef dinner prepared by Jon and Marie Nelson who had known

John Ottertail from their days at Beaverhouse Ranger Station several years previously, when John would stop in for permits for the fishing parties he guided.

Later, visiting Powell's Resort on Saganaga, eight miles east of Cache Bay, John exchanged many stories of the past with Dorothy Powell, widow of his cousin.

Leaving Saganaga, we portaged north past Silver Falls into Saganagons Lake, where John suddenly pointed ahead and said, "Six canoes from Lac La Croix camped there. In one canoe was Chief Kagike-gwa-neb with his family, six pups and two cats. I was only seven then, so it must have been in 1935...I remember also that my mother made maple sugar along the Maligne River -- at least a hundred pounds."

At the next portage we exchanged greetings with eight ladies from an "Over-40 Club." As Shan showed them some of Quetico's interesting plants, John explained about the piles of moose droppings along the trail. He was still laughing as he carried his packs to the end of the portage, saying, "Those ladies ask many, many questions!"

At Wet Lake we took pictures of his cousin's name, printed in black pitch on a smooth slab of granite bedrock -- "Mike Powell, 1918." Mike and his father, Jack, were Quetico Park fire rangers.

Battling a strong headwind, we inched up Kawnipi Lake past Kawa Bay, and McKenzie Bay, to the sheltered channel west of Rose Island, where John told how he spent three weeks alone there one fall while trapping. One night he heard wolves howling, one after the other, and the next day, the lake was frozen over. A week later, he left with 15 mink, two fisher, 16 beaver, and one otter.

That evening, at a lovely campsite on Kawnipi, I recorded two of my favourite Ojibwe words: a-ni-mi-gi ("thunder") and a-ni-mi-gi-mi-ga ("rainbow, or path of the thunder.") (see colour insert).

David Thompson, in 1798, recorded a visit with Ojibwe people, who, on seeing a rainbow after a storm, said, "Ah, we shall yet live -- there is the shaft of life."

After ten days of canoeing we were all feeling young and strong again, and the hill from Chatterton to Russell did not seem as high as we had remembered. It truly was a good trip with good people!

Frank Jordan, Jr., standing, with John Ottertail in the stern. At Russell Lake campsite.

Our trip was one of many events to mark the anniversary, which was shared by Superior National Forest. (It, too, was created in 1909.) Co-operative, cross-border celebrations included a 130-kilometre, Canada-U.S. ski trip, and an 11-day canoe journey from Lac La Croix to Grand Portage along the "Voyageurs Highway." An official 75th anniversary party was held simultaneously at Prairie Portage and Dawson Trail Campgrounds in July. Alan Pope, then Natural Resources minister, gave this message at Prairie Portage:

Thank you for your friendship in a common cause -- the wise management of one of the world's great natural areas.

We've been enjoying that camaraderie ever since 1910, when those first rangers from Minnesota and Ontario would often share the same cabin on cold winter nights along the border. Since then, they've patrolled for poachers and fought fires side-by-side and come to the aid of canoeists in each other's waters. In Quetico-Superior, our rule is take action first, figure out what country you're in later.

...What we have is a partnership that has worked well for 75 years and will continue to work well long after all of us are gone. It's the kind of co-operation that will help us solve mutual problems and manage resources wisely all along our particular stretch of the longest undefended border in the world.

What we have created together is a monument to co-operation -- an area that American conservationist Ernest Oberholtzer described as "a magic land..." But Oberholtzer, in his wisdom, also noticed something about Quetico-Superior that goes beyond the scenery and communities of wild living things -- he said: "It had a spirituality." ...[It is] a place to reflect and find renewal.

[Sig] Olson said that...the very presence of wilderness...is a balance wheel to civilization, a reminder of the basic problems of existence. The fact that here people can gain perspective and a sense of oneness with mountains, forests and waters enriches their lives, makes them better able to withstand the forces to which they must return."

The eight skiers who crossed Quetico Park from Atikokan to Ely arrive at the finish line. The four Canadians from Atikokan were: Jack Kosola, Bob Burns, Jim Hopper, and Dan Whaley.

Quetico-Superior 75th Anniversary celebration at Prairie Portage. Bill Ross, regional archaeologist, unveils the plaque commemeorating the Quetico-Superior.

Friends of Quetico Park inaugural board meeting on 18 April 1984. Pat Reid, MPP, 2nd on the left, was the guest of honor.

Another important event in the 75th anniversary year was the founding of the Friends of Quetico Park. The Friends' inaugural meeting was held in Atikokan in April 1984, when the group set out two objectives: to help preserve the park, and to encourage tourism and recreational activities in the Quetico-Atikokan area. The first board -- consisting of former Atikokan Reeve Syd Hancock, Don Beckett, Brian Morris, Dan Paleczny, Martha Stradiotto, Dave Bates, Jim Hopper, Marie Nelson, and Inga Hopper -- began the group's non-profit work.

Perhaps appropriate to 1984's historic theme, the year also saw the discovery of a new aboriginal pictograph north of Montgomery Lake. Eva Lake trapper Phil Sawdo found the images of moose, caribou and maymaygwayshi (mythical, leprechaun-like beings). This discovery was a timely reminder of Quetico's long human history.

Quetico Park Information Pavilion.

During this time, groundbreaking was held for the new Dawson Trail Visitor Centre. Designed by architect John Hix, the building (often called simply "The Pavilion") received an award from the Canadian Architect Awards Program. However, the Pavilion did not house the park headquarters, which relocated from the Nym Lake base to Atikokan.

When it was completed, the Pavilion became home to the John B. Ridley Research Library, a facility set up through a substantial grant from the Quetico Foundation. The library was named for the Foundation's former chairman, John Ridley, who oversaw the Foundation's charitable work for over 20 years. During his tenure, the Foundation funded a wide range of research activities at Quetico, and published eight books (including *Plants of Quetico*) detailing the results of that research. The Research Library officially opened in 1986 and was funded by the Quetico Foundation for the next ten years. Day-to-day library operations were taken over by the Park in 1997.

Andy Harjula became Atikokan District Manager in 1979. Here he is on the left in 1985 with Jack Bankes and Keith Reynolds from the Quetico Foundation.

Three drummers from Lac La Croix First Nation at Quetico Day, 27 July 1985. Bob Ottertail on the left, Bob Geyshick and Frank Jordan on the right.

Opening of the John B. Ridley Research Library, 26 July 1986. From left to right: Mrs. J. Bankes, Mrs. John B. Ridley, Jack Bankes (former chairman of the Quetico Foundation), Jane Dysart, Sandra Louet, and Dr. and Mrs. Keith Reynolds. Dr. Reynolds was Chairman of the Foundation.

Opening of the John B. Ridley Research Library, 26 July 1986. This group includes MPP Jack Pierce, Chief Steve Jourdain and District Manager Steve Toole on the right.

236

Lac La Croix School canoe trip, 1986. The trip was to Argo Lake and Darky Lake, returning down the Darky River to Minn Lake and McAree Lake. The purpose was to talk of their heritage and visit traditional places. Shirley Peruniak is second from left, standing.

Amelia Burnside, her daughter Marie Ottertail, Marie's son Kalvin and his wife with his wife's mother, Mrs. Geyshick. All at Lac La Croix Ranger Station with Joe and Vera Meany in the early 1980s.

Wilderness Voices: Shan Walshe

When Shan Walshe died in March 1991, the *Thunder Bay Times-News* called him the "conscience" of Quetico. In its 90-year history, few people have been as intimately associated with Quetico, or have worked harder for its preservation. The park held magic for him...Walshe once wrote: "The park's sparkling waters, mysteriously pictographed cliffs and vast natural forests are the essence of northern wilderness. Encountering these natural features in an isolated setting, I often experience the exhilaration of an explorer who has come upon them for the first time."

Shan is remembered for his love of nature; of plants and the story they tell; of geology and the minerals the rocks supply; of the animals that found a home here. Most of all, he loved to share what he had learned. In doing so, he won advocates for the wilderness he loved, where nature was able to teach its lessons.

Walshe's relationship with Quetico spanned more than 20 years. He became Quetico park naturalist in August 1970, having just completed studies in plant ecology at the University of Toronto. Believe it or not, Shan's first vocation wasn't ecology, but languages: he trained in and taught foreign languages for most of the 1960s.

From the first days of his Quetico assignment, Walshe blazed his own independent trail. He spent every available hour in the wilds, and strayed far from the paperwork of government. Former superintendent Dave Elder once commented wryly that Walshe had "...an incredible ability to avoid any kind of administrative work."

Mike Barker said: "I guess Shan had a lot of ideas about how we should get out and get to be part of the park. And that just hit right on with my line of thinking because I've always felt that the people in the field ought to be in the field. They should be in the bush not sitting around in a bunch of offices. He managed to parlay his job which formerly had been sort of flitting around Dawson Trail Campgrounds, into a system whereby he spent half of the ice free period, pretty well, paddling around in Quetico. I was in total agreement with that..."

Superintendent Jay Leather at the dedication ceremony at Shan Walshe Lake, summer 1992. [Photo by Shirley Peruniak]

Walshe loved to *explain* the wilderness -- the complex relationships between all the flora and fauna of Quetico were rendered clear to his audience. He had a limitless curiosity that led him to explore. His book, *The Plants of Quetico and The Ontario Shield*, remains as a tribute to all those years of travel, observation and research. He once wrote that the flowers seemed "...to be imploring house-bound folk to forsake TV sets, card games and all other man-oriented paraphernalia and contemplate, for a moment, the wonders of Nature. Let us gain proper perspective in life's rat race by heeding that call." Historians Gerald Killan and George Warecki wrote that Walshe's outstanding work made him "one of the essential custodians of the Ontario Wilderness tradition."

People were sometimes fooled by Shan's apparently frail, ascetic appearance. He could, and would, push himself to the limit. His trips often lasted far into the night on little food, leaving his friend, former Quetico Park ranger Bob Hayes, commenting that Walshe had "a tremendous stamina." Shan's travelling companions were often put to the test.

For seventeen years, Walshe actually lived in the park. The family -- including wife Margie and their children Bridget, Patrick, Shannon, and Kathleen -- shared a log cabin at French Lake, where Walshe could step out into the wilderness he loved so much. "There is no one characteristic that justly explains the Quetico's greatness," he wrote. "It is the kinship you feel with nature and the nearness of your primitive ancestral past."

When Shan died, well-known Canadian film director Norman Jewison commented that Shan "will be there on moonlit nights when we sit around the fire. He will be there when paddles dip through dark waters. He will be there when we gather wild mushrooms. He will be there when we pitch the tent and lie quietly in the darkness. He will be there when the sun rises through the mist and when it goes down behind the pines. He will be there when the wolves howl and all life begins and ends with the seasons. He will always be there!"

Jay Leather: 1987-Present

Jay Leather became the ninth superintendent of Quetico Park in June 1987. Having worked at Algonquin Provincial Park for three years, and having spent another eleven years as superintendent of Killarney Provincial Park (opposite Manitoulin Island), Leather brought great experience to Quetico as it was overtaken with one, dominant issue: the relationship between the park and the Lac La Croix First Nation.

Obviously, this issue did not arrive as a bolt from the blue. From the earliest days of Quetico's existence, the interaction between the Lac La Croix people and the park was complex, and sometimes difficult. In the past, the rights of First Nations people to use the resources of Quetico had been disputed -- in 1927, Walter Cain, the long-serving deputy minister of Lands and Forests, wrote that:

Jay Leather.

"*It is true that in the North West Angle Treaty of 1873, the Indians were given the right to pursue their avocation of hunting and fishing throughout the tract surrendered, but it was subject to exceptions as might be made from time to time in the way of land taken up for fuel, mining, lumbering, or other purposes. The preservation of the game and wildlife is one of the outstanding objects to be served in establishing a Park and their purpose will be defeated if we are to permit the Indians to traverse the water and hunt and fish at their will in these restricted areas.*"

Until the 1940s, Lac La Croix people had been strongly discouraged from using the land, and had been fined as poachers on several occasions. Not until 1949 did the province permit the creation of traplines in the northwestern part of Quetico. (Hunter Island was off-limits to trapping.)

In the 1950s and 1960s, the band was given a commercial fishing license for white fish and for sturgeon. However, the catches proved not commercially viable. Guiding for sportfishing proved to be the reserve's economic lifeline.

Helen Geyshick smoking deer meat at Threemile Lake in 1994.
[Zabe MacEachren Collection]

The question then became: can the people of Lac La Croix use motorboats in Quetico, an area intended to be a motor-free wilderness? Some said "no" -- this was inconsistent with preservation of Quetico and wilderness values. Others said "yes" -- motorized travel was necessary to the livelihood of the Lac La Croix people.

The balance between these two poles was made and remade several times. The first Quetico Park master plan permitted motors on certain waters (namely, Quetico, Beaverhouse, Wolseley, Tanner, Minn, McAree, French and Pickerel lakes, the Wawiag River, and the Maligne River, and parts of Lac La Croix) as a temporary measure, and banned motors throughout the rest of the park. The ban exemption was extended several times, and finally extended indefinitely in 1987. The band then sought greater motorized access, the right to cache boats and to land aircraft as part of their guiding activities.

This debate turned to bigger issues. By the late 1980s, the need to address the chronic economic and social problems of the Lac La Croix community was not in dispute. The province brought a new perspective to the debate following the election of the Rae government. In 1991, then-Minister of Natural Resources Bud Wildman formally apologized in the Ontario Legislature to the Lac La Croix people for their mistreatment by Ontario. The province acknowledged that past governments had not "responded positively" to the needs of the band, and set out to make amends.

In 1992, the band set out its position in the "Lac La Croix Amendment Proposal." The band argued that "as a community we support the preservation of the many Parks around us. Our belief system and lifestyle are, for the most part, consistent with the objectives of the park. However, we must also think about livelihoods for our people. As well, we wish to ensure that our children have the freedom to enjoy the remnants of a lifestyle that has for the most part been taken away."

The Lac La Croix band took the province to task over two main issues: the 'cancellation' of the former Kawa Bay reserve in 1915; and the "effective extinguishment" of the band's treaty rights as a result of the creation of Quetico. The band stated it did not wish to remain an "exception" to the administration of Quetico.

The Amendment proposal made a series of recommendations affecting guiding and trapping in the park. There were also long-term recommendations with far-reaching consequences for the park:

"The objectives and management plan for Quetico Provincial Park be amended to include the Ojibwe citizens of Lac La Croix First Nation as an integral part of the fabric of Quetico Provincial Park.

A concerted effort be made and a long-term process established to create long-term employment opportunities for Lac La Croix First Nation citizens within the programs, maintenance and management of Quetico Provincial Park.

A committee be established made up of representatives from the Ministry of Natural Resources and Lac La Croix First Nation to begin developing recommendations to the Minister of Natural Resources for the implementation of the above."

Specifically, the band asked for: a program of interpretation that would give the First Nations viewpoint of Quetico; a higher degree of participation in park management for the band; a program to train young people on the reserve for jobs in Quetico Provincial Park; and the relocation of the current Lac La Croix entry station to the reserve itself.

After several years of negotiations and intense debate, an agreement was signed between the province and the Lac La Croix First Nation in June 1994. The agreement was incorporated into the Revised Park Policy of 1995. The cornerstone of the revised policy was a statement of the "Governing Principles of the Lac La Croix Agreement of Co-existence":

> *The formal government-to-government relationship between Ontario and the Lac La Croix First Nation is guided by the following governing principles contained within the Agreement of Co-Existence:*
>
> *1. All governments in Ontario, provincial and First Nations alike, have a shared responsibility to preserve, protect and enhance lands and natural resources for the benefit of future generations.*
>
> *2. The creation of Quetico Provincial Park has partially severed the people of Lac La Croix First Nation from their sacrosanct relationship with their ancestral homeland, the social health of*

Mind, Body and Spirit which is attributable to their relationship with the land and the economic benefits derived from the land area.

3. *The Parties agree that in light of indignities suffered by the citizens of the First Nation, their displacement from their traditional homeland and the loss of significant economic opportunities due to the creation of Quetico Provincial Park, it is vital to foster and promote a cooperative government-to government relationship of co-existence which recognizes the First Nation as a co-decision-maker in accordance with the provisions of this Agreement in the Quetico Area while providing significant cultural, social and economic opportunities to the First Nation.*

4. *The First Nation must be an active and full participant in the future planning, development and management of the Quetico Area in accordance with the provisions of this Agreement and share in the economic benefits derived from that Area.*

5. *The maintenance of the wilderness values of Quetico Provincial Park is of paramount importance to the people of Ontario and is consistent with sustaining the cultural and social integrity of both the First Nation and the Park.*

6. *The Parties agree that courses of action must be developed and implemented to meet the First Nation's economic needs and aspirations while consistent with the wilderness values of Quetico Provincial Park.*

7. *The Parties recognize that the lands and resources of Quetico Provincial Park have always been relied upon to fulfil many of the economic needs of the First Nation but that Quetico Provincial Park cannot be relied upon to fulfil all of the economic development needs of the First Nation.*

8. *The Parties recognize that improved power boat and aircraft access by the First Nation, in the short term, to Quetico Provincial Park is critical for the First Nation to realize its economic development needs and viability.*

245

9. *The Parties agree, that in keeping with the principles outlined above, to work towards the elimination of power boat and aircraft access to Quetico Provincial Park.*

Cheryl Ottertail and Shirley Peruniak bringing the Quetico-Lac La Croix History Albums to the First Nation in November 1990.

Marie Ottertail, Lac La Croix First Nation elder and Quetico Interpreter with Quetico Park naturalist Victor Miller in 1993.

Harvey Jordan, Melvin Geyshick and Preston Atatise from the Lac La Croix First Nation were hired under a Provincial Environmental Youth Corps Program to work in Quetico with Chuck Miller, Quetico's interior co-ordinator during the summer of 1988 and 1989.

Many of the band's specific proposals were also met, including relocation of the entry station to the reserve. Superintendent Jay Leather said that he felt "ecstatic that we have a signed agreement that talks about a whole series of principles, and the community signing to the wilderness goal of this park...those wilderness goals contribute to their social, cultural and economic well being. The community is signing to a process that will eliminate mechanized recreation."

Chief Leon Jourdain and Natural Resources Minister Howard Hampton shaking hands at the signing of the Agreement of Co-existence between the Lac La Croix First Nation and the Ontario Ministry of Natural Resources in June 1994.

Jay Leather makes a presentation to Chief Leon Jourdain in the Roundhouse at Lac La Croix First Nation. This presentation was made at the time of the Signing of the Agreement in 1994. Natural Resources Minister Howard Hampton is at right.

Left to right: Lloyd Burridge, Elaine Jourdain, Shirley Peruniak, Leon Jourdain, and Jay Leather. Photo taken at the time of the signing of the Agreement of Co-existence between the Lac La Croix First Nation and the Ontario Ministry of Natural Resources in June 1994.

Jay Leather and Anna Burnside at the opening of the Lac La Croix First Nation Work Centre in 1996. It was named in memory of Larry Burnside, former Quetico Park-MNR liaison officer with the Lac La Croix First Nation.

Ontario Hydro lines bring power to the Lac La Croix First Nation in 1994. Previously they had received power from Minnesota.

250

New Lac La Croix Ranger Station near the site of the First Nation. The Station was opened in 1998. **[Photo by Michael Dawber]**

Into the '90s

While the Lac La Croix process was the most important event of the time -- maybe in the park's history -- there were many other changes to Quetico in the 1990s.

From 1987 to the present day, Superintendent Jay Leather has overseen many changes in how Quetico serves its visitors. The age has become one of technological wonder and re-training of staff was imperative.

The old battery-operated radio system was improved as solar power re-charged the batteries, and even gave power to lights and a few other modern conveniences. At Prairie Portage, a generating system was tried in the river running down into Basswood Lake to the east of the main flow.

The quota system was tested. Budgets were reduced. The staff were sometimes overwhelmed as fewer people tried to provide the service that visitors had come to expect. An extensive review of the quota system was undertaken, and further fine-tuning was done.

Upgrading of roads, camp sites, water systems, and the extension of electricity to some campsites, showers, and washing facilities all came to the Dawson Trail campground.

Spruce budworm created a dangerous situation at that site, as the dead trees became a fire hazard and endangered the safety of campers.

Park wardens Karen Mikoliew and Terry Johnson with volunteers Amanda Benedict and Ashley Spenceley by the old Beaverhouse tower cabin in 1999.

All parks in the province were brought under the aegis of a new organization, Ontario Parks, in 1994. While still a part of the Ministry of Natural Resources, Ontario Parks was set up to both manage and promote the park system. "The encouragement of economic benefits through tourism" was set out as one of four objectives for the provincial parks program -- acknowledging the fact that tourism was now the biggest, and most lucrative, industry on the planet.

As a result of legislative changes, revenue generated in provincial parks was allowed to stay in the park system, instead of going into the general coffers of the government. Parks were expected to cover 75 per cent of their own costs by the year 2000 -- Quetico attained financial self-sufficiency in 1997.

Joe and Vera Meany at the Lac La Croix Ranger Station, seen here in 1978. They worked at the entry station from 1971-72 and 1974-96.

The park system saw another sweeping review under the Harris Conservative government, which started the "Lands for Life" process. The purpose of this process was to determine the use of all lands held by the province in three large geographic areas -- basically, crown land lying within the area of the Canadian Shield, from southeastern Ontario to the Manitoba Border.

After several years of consultation and review, the Lands for Life process resulted in a report called "Ontario's Living Legacy." The report proposed the creation of 60 new parks and 273 new Conservation Reserves, as well as expansion of 44 other parks and one additional Conservation Reserve. No changes were made to Quetico as a result of this process.

Brian Luckman, Murray Watt and Barb Kronberg by a large white pine on the Cache to Lindsay Lake portage in 1989. Luckman, on faculty at the University of Western Ontario and was Scientific Co-ordinator for the Global Change Program of the Geological Survey of Canada. He was assisting dendrochronology studies in the Quetico-Superior region.

In 1999, the province revolutionized the park service by creating a new, high-tech campsite reservation service. Not only can the public call a toll-free number to reserve sites in more than 60 parks, visitors will eventually be able to choose campsites 'on-line' through the Internet. We've traveled a long journey from the telegraph and the steam engine!

The itinerant Quetico park headquarters made another reloca-tion: this time to offices in the town of Atikokan. The then-park head-quarters at Nym Lake was shut down, as was the fire base located there. The move to Atikokan underlined how important the park was to the

254

economy of Atikokan: in spite of criticism to the contrary, an economic study showed that Quetico generated more than $3 million in economic activity in the Atikokan district.

The nature and purpose of parks was debated -- and perhaps reinterpreted -- over the issue of fire. No-one can question that fire is a normal part of the ecological process in the boreal forest. Before anyone ever set foot in the territory of Quetico, fires sparked by lightning burned the forest until natural controls (like rain or lack of dead or dying trees, called fuel or fuel wood) kicked in. Fire plays a critical role in determining the long-term health of an ecosystem by recycling nutrients, stabilizing soil, preventing disease and creating suitable habitat for young trees and for wildlife. Some plants such as Jack pine are so dependent on fire that, without the intense heat, Jack pine cones cannot open for reproduction.

When fire suppression began in Quetico the nature of the forest began to change. It allowed a build-up of fuel from blowdown and insect damage, setting the stage for much larger and more dangerous fires (as happened in 1995 in Fire #141).

Jay Leather took up the question of the role of fire in a wilderness park, encouraging research, visiting Yellowstone after a major fire struck that park, and taking every opportunity to open the matter for discussion. The goal was to obtain permission to re-introduce fire, a natural process in the boreal forest, back into Quetico.

The fire question came to the fore in 1995, when the park was hit by one of its worst fires this century. A lightning strike in the Bird Lake area spawned a wildfire that burned over 25,000 hectares of land -- about five per cent of the park's surface area. Many red and white pine, some up to 300 years old, were torched.

In 1998, a Fire Plan was proposed in accordance with Quetico's wilderness goal: to permit carefully selected forest fire to burn in designated areas, and allow fire to fulfil its ecological role within the confines of health and safety. Obviously, this ran counter to 90 years of park history: protection of the forest from fire was one of the fundamental tenets of the Ontairo park system. In Aubrey White's 1909 recommendation of the Quetico Forest Reserve, protection of Quetico's timber from fire was his central theme.

Fort Frances Fire #141, as seen from the north shore of Cache Bay in August 1995. T.J. Lynham of the Canadian Forest Service said, "Fire 141 was one of the most intense crown fires that you would see in Ontario." [Photo by Janice Matichuk]

The question now is: does that goal have to be re-interpreted in light of our modern understanding of the forest ecosystem? Wildfires help create and sustain a checkered pattern of different forest communities in different life stages. A rich diversity of forest communities sustains an abundance of wildlife, and creates the special intrigue and beauty of a wilderness landscape.

The proposal went to the public, and was approved in August of that year. When a fire is reported, it will be studied and if it meets the guidelines of the Fire Plan, it may be left to burn. In June 1999, Quetico permitted its first Prescribed Natural Fire (PNF) to fulfil its natural ecological role. The fire was sparked by a lightning strike and began to burn an area seven hectares in size just north of Pulling Lake (on the park's southwestern side). Park staff and a Fort Frances fire crew monitored the fire as it grew to 31 hectares, before rainfall stopped its growth. The fire cleared the understory of a maturing red and white pine forest, creating a nutrient-rich soil bed for new seedling growth.

Nineteen ninety-nine saw the dedication of an outdoor "Teaching Place," built at Dawson Trail Campgrounds with the active participation of elders and staff from Lac La Croix First Nation. Interpreter Kalvin Ottertail worked with the elders to compose the words to go on a plaque for the building:

The Teaching Place

This building is known as the "Teaching Place." A place where one can experience and see Quetico. Aboriginal People come to life through oral stories and slide presentations. In this building we provide Natural Heritage and Cultural Programs for those who wish to educate themselves further about Quetico and the Aboriginal People. The significance of the building is that of the Aboriginal Round House. It is a full circle, with no beginning and no end. This shape resembles the circle of life. You begin learning in the womb of your mother until your departure to the spirit world. Often, wisdom, knowledge and experiences are shared within a Round House setting where you are required to speak from your heart.

At the dedication of the Teaching Place, the elders made the request that this building be used with respect at all times for the teachings passed on.

Also that summer, a huge windstorm caused an enormous blowdown in the Boundary Waters. On 04 July, a storm tracking towards Quetico touched the park's southern boundary through the Man Chain and Emerald Lake. What are called "straight line winds" of up to 140 kilometres an hour tore off treetops and, in many cases, blew down trees, roots and all. This blowdown affected 11 000 hectares in Quetico along the International Boundary between Prairie Portage and Knife Lake. Although this sounds quite large, the damage on the

American side was vast: 350 000 hectares were damaged in Boundary Waters Canoe Area Wilderness.

Teaching place at the Dawson Trail Campground, opened in 1999.

Former Quetico Ranger Art Madsen, aged 94, went through the storm. Art is a long-time resident on the Canadian side of Saganaga Lake whose association with the park goes back to the early 1930s. Art was taking his daughter to the Gunflint Trail so she could meet a plane in Duluth. He reached the U.S. landing on Saganaga Lake, and told her to "unload fast. I've got to wheel. When you see black clouds forming like that, it could mean a twister."

Art tells the story... "I could see it was coming fast and black clouds had a brown yellowish color under them. Lightning and thunder were flashing all around and wind was really getting up. After a few miles I was following along a rock wall as I know lightning will hit the highest part. Quick as a flash I did not see the lightning but one of the loudest thunder cracks I'd ever heard nearly knocked my ears off. Then I could see this grayish wall of cloud coming fast and knew it would really put down heavy rain. When I crossed by Powells' place the wind was so strong it was pushing rain horizontally. I was coming into the dock area very fast. My granddaughter rushed out and snubbed my bow

258

rope to the dock. Within minutes the waves became five feet. This was the worst storm in the memory of some old timers."

Kalvin Ottertail standing with Lac La Croix drummers in the round-house at their First Nation.

Left to right: Suzie (Art's daughter), Art Madsen and Janice Matichuk at Cache Point on the occasion of Art's 90th birthday in 1994. Janice Matichuk is the Ranger at the Cache Bay Ranger Station. In 1999, she was awarded the MNR P.R.I.D.E. (People Recognizing Innovation, Dedication and Enthusiasm) Service award.

Final Thoughts

The significance of protected wilderness becomes clearer as it becomes harder to find.

I remember the silence and listening to a father's story of his son being afraid of the silence at first.

Who does not remember the sunsets beyond the forest, every one different?

The Quetico wilderness is dominated by rock. We can see the beginning of a process as stage followed stage until the rocks were covered in forest.

There is much to observe and to learn. We have the opportunity to return to the natural world and to deal with basic needs: shelter, warmth and food. In doing this we can forget the stresses of everyday life. It is a process for us of re-creation, perhaps the true meaning of the word.

Knowing the history of Quetico allows us a glimpse into the history of Canada. Perhaps we can hear the voices of the past in the wind as it sings through the pines.

Here the values of aboriginal society and of white society are merging to ensure that there will be a wilderness to pass on to our children and to their children. Knowing the past, they will want to honor, respect and take care of it.

Quetico's people become "spirits from the past" whose stories are enacted as reminders of how rich this history is and how it tells a story of Canada.

The faster modern life whirls, the more necessary will be the unspoiled corners of the globe.

Selected References:

- Bertrand, J.P. Highway of Destiny : an Epic Story of Canadian Development. New York : Vantage Press, 1959.
- Bjorkman, Sylvia. Wilderness Wealth 1899-1999 : Atikokan and Surrounding Areas. 1998.
- Campbell, Marjorie Wilkins. The North West Company. Toronto : Macmillan Co., 1957.
- Dawson, S.J. Report on the Exploration of the Country Between Lake Superior and the Red River Settlement. Greenwood Press, 1968. First published in 1859 by order of the Legislative Assembly, Toronto, Appendix 36.
- Denis, Keith. Canoe Trails Through Quetico. Toronto : The Quetico Foundation, 1959.
- Henry, Alexander. Travels and Adventures in Canada and the Indian Territories Between the years 1760 and 1776. Readex Microprint, 1966. Facsim. of: New York : I. Riley, 1809.
- Hind, Henry Youle. Narrative of the Canadian Red River Exploring Expedition of 1857 and of the Assinniboine and Saskatchewan Exploring Expeditions of 1858. London, England : Longman, Green, Longman and Roberts, 1860.
- International Boundary Commission. Joint Report Upon the Survey and Demarcation of the Boundary Between the United States and Canada from the Northwesternmost point of Lake of the Woods to Lake Superior. Washington, D.C. Government printing Office, 1931.
- Killan, Gerald. Protected Places : a History of Ontario's Provincial Parks System. Toronto : Dundurn Press, 1993.
- Lake Names of Quetico Provincial Park. Atikokan, Ont. : Friends of Quetico Park, 1992.
- Lambert, Richard S., with Paul Pross. Renewing Nature's Wealth. Ontario Dept. of Lands and Forests, 1967.
- Litteljohn, Bruce. Quetico-Superior Country : Wilderness Highway to Wilderness Recreation. Toronto : The Quetico Foundation, 1965. Originally published in Canadian Geographical Journal August and September 1965.
- Litteljohn, Bruce. The Dawson Route : a Phase of Westward Expansion. Unpublished M.A. thesis, University of British Columbia, 1967.

- Mackenzie, Alexander. Voyages from Montreal in the River St. Lawrence Through the Continent of North America to the Frozen and Pacific Oceans in the years 1789 and 1793 with a Preliminary Account of the Rise, Progress, and Present State of the Fur Trade of that Country. 1927. Reprint of: London : Printed for T. Cadell, Jun. and W. Davies, Strand; Corbett and Morgan, Paul Mall; and W. Creech, at Edinburgh; by R. Nobe, Old-Bailey, 1801.
- Morse, Eric W. Fur Trade Canoe Routes of Canada : Then and Now. Toronto : University of Toronto Press, 1979.
- Nute, Grace Lee. The Voyageur's Highway : Minnesota's Border Lake Land. St. Paul, Minn. : Minnesota Historical Society, 1941.
- Oberholtzer, Ernest C. Diaries of Quetico Canoe Trips 1909, 1910. Oberholtzer Foundation.
- Olson, Sigurd F. The Singing Wilderness. New York : Alfred A. Knopf, 1956.
- Quetico Provincial Park Revised Park Policy, 1995. Ontario Ministry of Natural Resources, 1995.
- Pages from the Past. Atikokan, Ont. : Friends of Quetico Park, 1992.
- Searle, Newell R. Saving Quetico-Superior : a Land Set Apart. St.Paul. Minn. : Minnesota Historical Society, 1977.
- Tanner, John. The Falcon : a Narrative of the Captivity and Adventures of John Tanner. Toronto : Penguin Books, 1994. Originally published: G. & C. & H. Carvill, 1830.
- Walshe, Shan, assisted by Shirley Peruniak. Saga of the Quetico-Superior Wilderness, 1909-1984 : 75 years of International Co-operation. Quetico Provincial Park, 1984.
- Warecki, George. The Quetico-Superior Council and the Battle for Wilderness in Quetico Provincial Park, 1909-1960. Unpublished M.A. thesis, University of Western Ontario, 1983.
- Warecki, George. Protecting Ontario's Wilderness : a History of Wilderness Conservation in Ontario, 1927-1973. Unpublished Ph.D. thesis, McMaster University, 1989.